Small Talk in Wiltshire

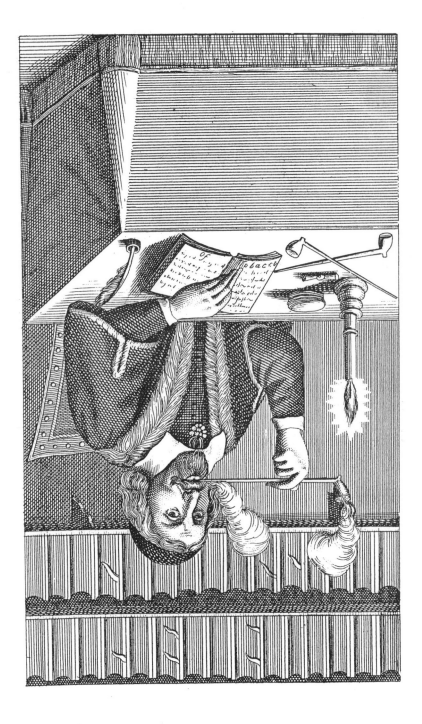

Small Talk in Wiltshire

wherein are Discover'd sundry *Endeavours*
(Literary and Otherwise)
by Wiltshire *Men* and *Women* chiefly
during the *Eighteenth* and *Nineteenth* Centuries,
together with certain *Mishaps* which *befell* them.

collected and *presented* by

John Chandler

Ex Libris Press

First published in 1992 by
Ex Libris Press
1 The Shambles
Bradford on Avon
Wiltshire

Typeset in 10 point Century Schoolbook and Palatino

Design and typesetting by Ex Libris Press

Cover Printed by Shires Press, Trowbridge
Printed and bound in Great Britain by
Cromwell Press Ltd., Broughton Gifford, Wiltshire

ISBN 0 948578 32 7

Source of illustrations

Frontispiece – Edward Duke: *The Halle of John Halle*, extra illustrated copy;
p. 13 – view of Trowbridge from John Britton: *Beauties of Wiltshire, vol. 2*, 1826;
pp. 28 & 91 – Wiltshire characters from W.H.Hudson: *A Shepherd's Life*: Methuen,
1910; p. 34 – Broughton Gifford church from *Church Rambler*, 1878; pp. 45 &
104 – drawings by Thomas Rowlandson; p. 51 – John Britton: *Beauties of Wiltshire,
vol. 2*, 1826; p. 53 – John Hissey: *Through Ten English Counties*, 1894; p. 59 –
C.G.Harper: *The Bath Road*, 2nd. ed., 1923; p. 62 – *The Highwaymen of Wiltshire*,
c. 1845; p. 64 – W. Fletcher: *Steam on Common Roads*, 1891; p. 67 – *Life and
Poetical Works of George Crabbe by his son*, 1901; p. 72 – John Britton: *Autobiography, vol. 1*, 1850; pp 75 & 77 – *WAM, vol. 1*; p. 85: *Chamber's Encyclopaedia*;
p. 98 – P. Hall: *Picturesque Memorials*; p. 115 – Edward Hutton: *Highways and
Byways in Wiltshire*, 1917; p. 112 – Howard Swinstead: *A Parish on Wheels*, 1897.

Contents

Preface

It has been my privilege to have spent much of my working life so far, day in and day out, among the literature and records of local history. In doing so I have observed that, although some books on the library shelf are consulted almost daily, there are many others on whose top edge the dust thickens in desuetude. But somebody wrote them, somebody took the trouble to print them, and somebody must once have bought them, and perhaps even read them. Each has a story to tell – whether it now appears silly or earnest, misguided or dull, obsolete or obscure.

The same thought should strike anyone who scans old newspapers. In among the advertisements for cocoa, the Parliamentary intelligence and the shocking accidents, the prospector will occasionally find nuggets of pure gold. And every now and then, among some dryasdust documents in the record office, a human being surmounts the barrier of centuries to communicate, in language we all understand.

While I have been compiling this little book I have described it to my friends as an anthology, but I see now that I should rather have called it a sampler. It only scratches the surface of a vast, and largely untapped and uncharted, resource. In the manner of samplers it is intended for dipping into, and has no very rigid structure. But it does, assuredly, have a model.

Cecil Torr wrote *Small Talk at Wreyland*, he tells us, for private circulation among his personal friends. But he was persuaded to publish it, and the first part appeared in 1918. It takes the form of apparently random thoughts and reminiscences, by a genial scholar, who chose to cocoon himself in the house which he inherited in a hamlet on the edge of Dartmoor – this hamlet, incidentally (a learned friend tells me), should be pronounced 'Relland'. Much of his writing is autobiographical, but there are also long extracts from the diaries and correspondence of his father and grandfather, two canny Victorian squires. These extracts, concerning foreign travel, local events and much besides, are presented more or less at random, and are accompanied by Torr's own comments.

Such a gentle, bumbling, approach to the past seemed to me to be the perfect vehicle for presenting a selection from the kind of material which I have described; and in my own inadequate way I have tried to follow Torr's example – even to the extent of shamelessly borrowing part of his title. But there is little autobiography here, and I have neither the wit, nor the charm nor wisdom which makes Torr's book so special. In compiling it, however, I have enjoyed myself enormously; and if a fraction of the fun which went into the writing, comes across in the reading, I shall be more than satisfied.

It remains for me to thank most heartily the usual crew who never seem to complain about the inconveniences which my researches cause them. That is to say: Steven Hobbs and his colleagues in the Wiltshire Record Office; Michael Marshman, Felicity Gilmour and Wendy Bate in the Trowbridge Local Studies Library (Wiltshire County Council, Library and Museum Service); and Pamela Colman and Lorna Haycock in the Library of the Wiltshire Archaeological and Natural History Society at Devizes. I should like to offer my more formal thanks to the Wiltshire Archaeological and Natural History Society, the Wiltshire Record Office and the Wiltshire County Council Library and Museum Service for allowing me to use material in their possession. Finally, I am grateful to Ken Rogers for a number of leads, Roger Jones for his (probably misguided) confidence in publishing this collection, and my wife, Alison Borthwick, who once again has had to put up with my anti-social behaviour, and then has cheerfully and critically read the outcome.

John Chandler
East Knoyle
September 1992

I n t o P r i n t

Prefaces and Other Mishaps

Did you read my preface? I mention it only because some people tend to skip the preface and begin straight away with the book. Myself, I tend to read the preface and not bother with the book – but I imagine that this must be a bad habit picked up as a librarian. Prefaces can be a problem, certainly, for the writer as well as the reader. Take Edward Duke, for example, who in December 1836 sat down to crown the first volume of his literary achievement, *Prolusiones Historicae, or Essays illustrative of the Halle of John Halle*, (John Halle being a merchant of Salisbury) with a fourteen-page preface:

> This, almost constituent, portion of a book is presumed to be the first written, but (as in the present instance) it is, generally, the expiring efforts of the author's pen. It is, in reality, his postscript.
> It often serves to develope the style, and character, of the book itself, and is an index to the mind of its author...

Yes, that is where the problems begin. No-one is at their best while expiring, and a book all too candidly reveals the mind – and limitations – of its author. In this first chapter we shall conduct a little survey of some of the also-rans of Wiltshire history, and may discover some of the hurdles aspiring authors have to surmount.

Perhaps the first lesson to be learnt is that, if you are at all doubtful about tiresome matters like syntax and spelling, you ought to ask someone to look your manuscript over for you, before you send it to the printer. Good advice, but not always heeded. Take John Watts, for example, who in 1860 published his seven-page life story, *Self Help: the autobiography of Mr. John Watts, of Heytesbury, Professor of Gardening and Education.* Here is a sample:

daved Rose from a shepherd boy to a king and I rose from a shepherd boy to garddener. I head now eduction and if I make eney stake you must Exquese me. I do not now Eney thing bout grammer, I now more bout my granfather. My granfather wher very claver man. He meade villen [? a violin] out of old tailbord. I have herd pepel seay the did reember befre the wher born – the did rember hering the kees rattle in ther mothers pocket. I can not rember so long is theat, I can rember hering my mother seay that I was such a monster the coud Put me in to teapot. I never walk for 3 years, I walk at last From a goosbery tree to goosbery tree to fiend wich was the best, and was black one.

Once you are happy with your literary style there is the matter of illustrations to consider. There is always the danger that you may upset some of your readers if the pictures are not entirely suitable. And a hitch at this stage can disrupt the entire publishing schedule. Take this advertisement, for instance, which appeared in a local newspaper in 1767.

This Day is Published, Price 1s. A Plain Narrative of Facts, relating to the Person who lately passed under the assumed Name of the Princess Wilbrahama, lately detected at the Devizes; containing her whole History, from her first Elopement from the Hon. Mrs Sc——t's, till her Discovery and Commitment to Devizes Bridewell: Together with the very extraordinary Circumstances attending that Discovery, and the Report of a Jury of Matrons summoned on that Occasion.

In this Account will be found some Circumstances, which seem remarkably to corroborate the so much disputed Reality of the Caenean Metamorphosis and Androgynian Mystery of the Ancients; and some Hints which tend to explain the celebrated Gryph of Bononia...

London: Printed for the Author; and sold by the Booksellers in Great Britain and Ireland.

NB. Some Caracatures being thought necessary to elucidate particular Parts of this History, the Author has taken all possible Care to engage the best Artists for that Purpose.

TO THE PUBLIC – The directions given by the Draughtsman to the Engraver, occasioned some of the Caricatures in the Memoirs of the Princess Wilbrahama to be too indelicately express'd, and as there have been no more than half a dozen yet delivered out, and those too, among the Author's particular friends, hopes the public will excuse the delay of the publication, till the latter end of next month; when two other prints shall be inserted, that shall not in the least offend delicacy. NB. The Author likewise hopes, that those Gentlemen who have in possession those half dozen already published, will, for the above reasons, carefully lay them aside.

Nowadays that kind of tactic is known as 'hype', and is very effective. But there is always the danger that one of your friends with the unexpurgated version will sell the story to a Sunday newspaper. Just imagine the headline – FAKE ROYAL IN SEX-CHANGE ROW: SHOCK REVELATIONS.

*　　*　　*

A *Librarian's* Treachery

No such vulgarities in the past, of course, but you still had to be careful of your friends. James Bodman, who published the first ever history of Trowbridge, in 1814, had a very unhappy experience with his librarian, a Mr Wearing. Fuelled by envy, according to Bodman, Wearing had inserted an advertisement for Bodman's book in the *Bath Herald*, but had included in it a number of misprints and errors, so as to make its author look ridiculous. So angry was Bodman, that he wrote a special poem on the subject, and included it as an epilogue to his book:

A POEM

When some of the wise heads had learn'd my intention,
To publish a work without their own invention;
To stop my proceeding, they held a consultation,
How they might succeed to stop my publication.

One said, "Twill be in vain to attack him directly,
'But if we assail him, let's do it correctly,
'And before he gets ready, we'll publish his work,
'But to accomplish our purpose, in secret we'll lurk.

'But to accomplish our work we cannot well find
'A pretext, by which we may publish his mind:
'But the way to betray him, to answer our end,
'We'll feign to applaud him, as being his friend.'

But who can accomplish this wicked intention,
To cut a man's throat by a friendly pretension?
'Why I,' says Smooth Looks, 'I'll sign my name W——g,
"Tis part of my office, for I'm your librarian.'

A note he then wrote, pretending as friend,
To obtain such an answer as might suit their end.
'To complete my design on the man, as reverer,
'I'll employ one to publish, my friend Mr.Meyler.'

'Well said, my friend W.G., the business is done,
'Send down his own paper to Meyler and Son,
'Say, "Print it verbatim, but in any wise,
'Put many false letters, the work stigmatize.'"

At length, like the panther, who misses his prey,
And leaps to his thicket to avoid a just flay;
He writes and says, 'He's not alone a hooper;'*
But if I think well, I may fall on a Cooper.

---

* Where the panthers inhabit, they are called Hoopers, because they
betray the traveller by imitating the human voice.

Early nineteenth century view of Trowbridge

All a Matter of Confidence

One cannot help feeling that James Bodman was quite capable of making himself appear ridiculous, without any assistance from Mr Wearing. Perhaps part of the trouble was that he lacked confidence. This comes over in his preface:

> But let me take leave to say, that to write a first History, is like a mariner going to sea without a rudder or compass, or one travelling by night in some trackless country, who has a certain object to go to, without light or path. But if I am so fortunate as to bring but a glimmering light out of this gross darkness, I hope the next attempt will be exceedingly visible; especially if undertaken by an abler hand. I do not expect to fare better than authors who are well qualified for publishing – I do not expect to escape the sneers or reproaches of the envious man, or the find fault reader; who (to use the words of a great writer) is like a growling dog over his viands, who very often snarls and growls over that very food by which he is satisfying himself, and filling his stomach...

What he needed was a stirring title-page, something to intrigue and impress the potential reader. How about this:

> Warminster Common: shewing the steps by which it has advanced from its former state of notorious vice, ignorance, and poverty, to its present state of moral and social improvement... to which is added, an account, never before published, of numerous and important cures performed by that wonderful agent, Medical Electricity. By W. Daniell... 1850.

Or, even better, something to show that you are an author of considerable accomplishments:

Swindon Fifty Years Ago (More or Less). Reminiscences, Notes, and Relics of ye Old Wiltshire Towne, by Master William Morris, Author of 'France and the French', 'Ireland and the Irish', 'In Search After Ozone and Oblivion', 'Out and Home Again by way of Canada and the United States', 'What a Summer's Trip told me of the People and the Country of the Great West', Etc., Etc. Reprinted from ye Swindon Advertiser. Swindon: Printed and Published by the Author, at the 'Advertiser' Office, 10, Victoria Street.

No-one is left in any doubt that Master William Morris was a man of the world. But William Morris (not to be confused with his more famous namesake) was a journalist, you see, and journalists are concerned to make an impact.

Some authors, however, no matter how important the things they have to say, shun all publicity and live the life of a recluse. John Legg of Market Lavington published two important treatises in 1780, on bird migration and on the grafting of plants. Both appeared anonymously, and Legg's achievements would never have been credited to him at all were it not for renewed interest in his work during the 1890s, and the quest to discover his true identity.

The help of Alfred Smith, doyen of Wiltshire ornithologists, was enlisted, and after considerable frustration he not only discovered a memorial tablet to Legg in Market Lavington church (he died in 1802, aged 47), but also made contact with surviving members of his family. As a result he was able to paint this vignette of a private, tortured soul:

He lived and died a bachelor, and for some time at least, if not to the end of his short life, his sisters lived with him. He appears to have had no profession, but to have devoted himself in his early years to the study of Nature; and he is reported by his descendants to have practised the art of grafting and inoculation of trees in his own garden at

Lavington: but in the latter part of his life, for he died in middle age, he was absorbed in religious speculations; and he appears to have latterly given way to melancholy thoughts and unhappy broodings, to which he was doubtless predisposed by much infirmity of body. Family tradition reports that towards the end of his life he shut himself up almost completely, seldom moving beyond his garden, where he indulged in reveries, and mused in solitude: nay, so persistently did he shun the society of his fellows that he objected to be seen in the village street, and to avoid observation he is said to have made a private path to the Church, by which he could go unseen by any: and even when a young relative was taken by her mother to visit him, all she ever saw of the recluse was his pigtail as he darted upstairs to avoid the interview. His nephew, too, recorded that he never saw him but once, and that then he never spoke to him.

* * *

A Cynic

A few months before John Legg's birth, and a few miles away in Devizes, an author of a very different kind published an anonymous book. *Origines Divisianae, or the antiquities of the Devizes: in some familiar letters to a friend, wrote in the years 1750, and 1751*, was probably the first 'spoof' local history ever written, and I can only think of one other since, Osbert Lancaster's, *Drayneflete Revealed*. The author's cynical approach is summed up in an anecdote, with which he opens his second letter:

An old woman, who shew'd Lord Bathurst's fine place by Cirencester, was ask'd by a Gentleman that came to see it – Pray what building is that? – Oh, Sir, that is a ruin a thousand years old, which my Lord built last year; and he proposes to build one this year half as old again.

The book's author was a certain James Davis, a Devizes physician, and its printer claimed that by the time it was published in 1754 the author was dead (although the *Dictionary of National Biography* states that he died on 13th July 1755 – so perhaps that, too, was just his little joke). Davis was a cynic, and the target of his book was the improbable antiquarian speculations of William Stukeley and his coterie. He was well aware of their learned footnote technique, so he includes his own parody:

(a) The uncommon advantages of Etymological knowledge you will find very handsomely handled by a Friend of mine in his ingenious treatise on Barley Wine; who is a merry Greek, and sensible even when Carotic or Carybaric; and indeed always, but when he is delicate, v. Oinos Krithinos, p.23, and a dissertation upon Close-stools.

A close-stool, incidentally, was what we should call a commode. But the most cutting satire is kept for the list of contents, which is printed at the end of the book:

LETTER 1: A Preamble of a School-boy — A peep at a Town and a Castle — A doubt whether it be British, Roman or Saxon — Julius Caesar knew nothing of it, that's poz — Musgrave mistaken, St-k—y mistaken, every body mistaken but the Author — Monks were good scholars — Roman coins and Penates found here — Why they were hid — Mr. Wise hinted to be otherwise.

LETTER II: A Speech of an old Woman on Ruins — Roger Poor Bishop of Salisbury. suddenly metamorphiz'd into poor Roger — King Stephen a Pretender — Alexander Bishop of Lincoln a son of a whore — Henry Blois Bishop of Winchester an ecclesiastical Bully — His brother King Stephen a pickpocket.

LETTER III: Fitzhubert an errant Freethinker — Dy'd in his shoes — The Castle not heard of for 100 years, being hid all that time in a mist — A pause in the narration for a muzzy description — A long tedious Story about Hubert de Burgo Lord Chancellor — How he had like to have been kidnapp'd and how he conjur'd himself thro' a Keyhole into a Monastry — Henry the third out at Elbows — Account of a Trap-door near the High-Altar in Merton Priory very convenient for prime Ministers in the Suds [i.e. in trouble] — A dispute between Captain Geoffry Crancomb and an honest sturdy anonymous Blacksmith — Henry the third not quite so bold a pickpocket as King Stephen — Hubert had nothing to live upon, but bread; water, and his beads, for he would not eat his own words — Peter de Rupibus Bishop of Winchester had a heart as hard as a stone — Robert Bishop of Salisbury sent some Constables to the Devil — Hubert conveyed miraculously to Wales and never heard of after.

LETTER IV: A pair of new fashion'd spectacles recommended to all Antiquarians — Cambden an old fashion'd wary precise Antiquarian — A description of a fine place of ruins — Digressions of use to Authors and booksellers — Castles dye of consumptions — The most antique pair of scales, ever known, try'd — St—k—y almost lost in a Roman ditch of his own making.

And so on, and so on.

But whether such a display of wit and erudition impressed its audience and damaged its victims is hard to assess. Davis is virtually unknown now, and his book very scarce, whereas Stukeley figures large in every history of archaeology – even though much of what he believed was absurd, as Davis realized.

*   *   *

A Two-edged Sword

And here's another matter which the budding author should bear in mind. If you wish your books to be a publishing success you should try to include somewhere an indication that they will impress their audience. Choice snatches from as many favourable reviews as possible is the best way.

But do make sure that they are favourable. Edward Duke published a prospectus for his book on John Halle, which included the following reviews:

> This work deserves a place amongst the curiosities of literature – *John Bull.*

> We know not when we have met with a more amusing publication than the first volume of a work entitled the Halle of John Halle – *Bristol Journal.*

> This work will be esteemed by those who like to make the history of manners auxiliar to the history of events and persons. Most heartily indeed do we 'throw our old shoe' after it – *Literary Gazette.*

It is probably a mistake to publish extracts from reviews of your work, unless you are absolutely sure that they are meant to be genuinely complimentary. Anyone who has experience of reviewing local history books, and who has tried to be gentle on a second-rate work so as not to discourage its aspiring author, will know what I mean, and will be able to read between the lines of a review. The back-handed compliment is a favourite device, and I remember once having it done to me: 'The author analyses his material in ways that a modern historian would approve of...' – and I too made the mistake of quoting it on the fly-leaf. Since then I have paid similar compliments to others.

Edward Slow, the dialect poet from Wilton, whose work we shall sample later, was fond of including press notices in his books. But when we read this accolade of his poetry from *Public Opinion* – 'his skill with the West country lingo is curious and interesting' – or this, from the *Durham Chronicle* – 'It is not high-class poetry, certainly; but it does not come below the average...' – we may comment 'Two cheers'. Worse, from Slow's point of view, is his use of the review in *Court Circular*, which he quotes thus:

His poems are certainly very amusing, * * * Mr Slow also

writes in English, and his verses have the true ring of feeling in them.

The trouble is, that it does not take a great deal of imagination to guess the gist of the comment concealed by * * *.

*   *   *

Envoi
___

So, now we have covered the title page, the list of contents, the preface, the illustrations, the problems of editing, and all the publicity. There is just one more thing – the ending. Here is the closing passage from Edward Duke's epic volume, with which we began:

'Oh! my book, what shall I say unto thee? Oh! *mi ocelle!* thou apple of mine eye! thou little knowest the troubles, which too probably await thee! Thou art about to enter into life – about to encounter the passing remarks of those, who might meet thee in thy wandering path; and whilst, mayhap, some may kindly take thee by the hand, and send thee on thy way rejoicing, others may be intent on spying out all thy faults, and yield thee a more unfavourable reception. Thou mayest, in thy adventurous course, fall in with the grim critic, who, eyeing thee askaunt, *torvo vultu, truculentoque corde* [with a scowling face and a ferocious heart], may cleave thy skull with his literary tomahawk, or mercilessly plunge his sharpened knife into thy very heart. Thou art about to sail on a sea beset with rocks, and quicksands, and liable to encounter the tempestuous gale, which may hurl thee to inevitable destruction. Oh! my book! my anxious heart beats heavily for thy fate. Fare thee well! I can only add, in the words of Martial, *'I, fuge, sed poteras tutior esse domi'*.

Martial was probably right. His line can be roughly translated: 'Go, fly, but you could be safer staying at home.'
Actually, this passage is only the end of volume one... But volume two was never published.

Superstitions

A Donkey to the Rescue

Among the reminiscences of William Morris, the worldly wise newspaper proprietor, was the following little story:

I once had a donkey.
The other day I passed in the High-street, Swindon, a woman who once had a baby.
I always think of my donkey and her baby when I see that woman.

It is not very many years ago when, one day, I was called away from my books and papers to a woman with a baby in her arms at my door. The poor child was black in the face, and its body and limbs were perfectly rigid as it lay in its mother's arms in the throes of a fearful phlegmatic struggle.

'Oh please sir, I hope that you won't be offended by my asking, but would you let me pass my baby under your donkey's belly? It has the whooping cough so bad, and I am told that is the only way to cure it,' piteously exclaimed the woman as I neared her.

'How many times has it to be done?' I asked in reply, as it at once occurred to me that I had previously heard something of this remedy, with some vague idea that the ceremony had to be performed altogether nine times – three days in succession: then an interval of three days: then another passing for three days, and so on, until the child had been passed nine times under the donkey's belly on nine separate days, extending over a period of fifteen days, which, it must be admitted, was long enough time to either kill or cure the unfortunate patient.

'Only once, if you please, sir; but I must pass it under

the belly three times. You won't mind my doing it, will you, sir?'

In this year of grace, eighteen eighty-five, the mother of that child is, probably, still under forty years of age. I often see her in our streets, but I have never had the heart to ask her what the effect of her passing her child three times under the belly of my donkey had.

*   *   *

The Medicine Chest

William Morris was not alone in his concern to record old customs and beliefs. In the case of his native Swindon the contrast between old and new was more pronounced than elsewhere, naturally, since in 1885 most of Swindon was less than fifty years old; but similar attempts to collect information about the 'old ways' were made in many places. Folk cures were a case in point, because everywhere they were succumbing to the onslaught of scientific medicine.

Well, not quite everywhere. Here is Alfred Smith again, the ornithological detective, wearing a different hat, as he describes a bit of medical misunderstanding:

But to mark the supreme indifference to reason, and the mere working of a charm, which is really the light in which many of our rustics regard the prescriptions of medical men, I will give the following case, which occurred within my own personal knowledge, within the limits of the borough of Devizes. A labourer, being confined to his bed with a rather sharp attack of pleurisy, was visited by the parish doctor, who, together with other remedies, said he would send a blister [i.e. a poultice], which should be at once applied to the patient's chest. On the following day, when the medical gentleman visited his patient, he was met at the door by the sick man's wife, who, with great glee, expressed her admiration at the effects of the blister, which had done wonders; and said that her husband was in consequence much the better. The doctor of course expressed his satisfaction, but when he came to examine the sick man, he was surprised to find no trace of a blister, and on enquiring how that was, the wife with great readiness explained, 'You see, Sir, he hadn't got no chest, but he's got a good-sized box in the corner, and we clapp'd en on that': and there, sure enough, on a deal box, was the blister which had worked such a magic cure, to the no small merriment of the doctor.

* * *

Who needs a Doctor?

Such were the wonders of Victorian medical science. But to return to the older, traditional, treatments, we find that between 1893 and 1897 a series of cures was sent in by correspondents to the editor of a new journal, *Wiltshire Notes and Queries*, with a view to preserving and comparing them:

For the Gout, Rheumatism, or any other Defluction. Take polipody of the oak, hermodactyls, China root, sarsaparilla, of each four ounces, guaicum six ounces. Bruise these and infuse them 24 hours in 9 pints of water and 3 pints of white wine, in a pot close cover'd, haveing stood infusing 24 hours on a moderate fire; then let them boil gently to the consuption of a fourth part, and strain for use.

The same ingredients will serve again to make two more decoctions, pouring on them each time 6 pints of water and 2 of white wine, boiling and straining the liquor as before.

Drink for 3 days as much of this as reasonable as you can, the more so as not to be offended at it, the sooner will be the cure effected; while you drink of it abstain from broths, salads, sauces, fruits, fish, milk or anything made with it. N.B. You may eat of any sort of well roasted meat which is right easy of digestion and not salted. On every fourth day take a gentle purge, and while you take the decoction forbear all other liquors.

If you follow these directions exactly, you'l not fail of a cure in either gout or rheumatism or a sciatica; be sure you neglect not purging, otherwise you'l be apt to break out into boils.

This medicine greatly purifies the blood and only works by urine, and is an alterative only, and can be of no ill consequence to the patient. N.B. This has at once taking cur'd the most inveterate gout.

Observe: Not to put in the wine as menc'oned in the first paragraph, but filter the decoction and then put in the wine and give it two or three gentle boils.

Now, just wait a minute – that's not fair. Forgive me for interrupting, but you really cannot change your mind at this late stage in the recipe. We had enough trouble finding the hermodactyls, and by now we have been infusing our decoction for 24 hours.

Oh, well, you had better carry on with the next one, I suppose:

Snail Broth:- I knew two persons who were dosed with snail broth; it was used as a cure for consumption and wasting complaints. One of the patients was a young woman living at Bishopstrow, the other was a lad whose home was in Wales. The black, shell-less slugs that come out at night when the dew falls on the grass were also recommended to be eaten for the same disease, and I have been told by old folks now living in south Wilts that they have known many who partook of them. But for the snail broth I can myself vouch. The broth was made by boiling the snails, shells and all, in milk, straining it, and giving it to the sick person fasting, generally before breakfast. It was very slimy and jellied when cold. As children, we used to amuse ourselves by picking up the snails and singing-

> *Snail, snail, put out your horns,*
> *Or else I'll kill you.*

Or-

> *Snail, snail, come out of your hole,*
> *Or else I'll beat you as black as a coal.*

A Cure for Neuralgia:- Walking through one of the adjacent villages the other day I came across a farmer that I knew – a genuine son of the soil – and in response to his kind inquiries for my health, I complained to him that I had been sadly troubled with neuralgia of late. 'That is a sort of toothache,' said he, 'a thing I never had since I was a boy, and I will tell you what cured me. Old John, who has been dead this forty years, told me of it. Cut a piece off each finger- and toe-nail, and a piece off your hair, and get up on the next Sunday morning before sunrise and with a gimlet bore a hole in the first maiden-ash you come across and put the nails and hair in, then peg the hole up.'

A maiden-ash, for the benefit of your readers who would like to try the experiment, is an ash that has not been pollarded or topped.

Curious Recovery of Speech. ...a curious case is given by Archdeacon Squire of a person who, after having been dumb for years, recovered the use of his speech by means of a dream of this description:-

'One day, in the year 1741, he got very much in liquor, so much so that on his return home at night to Devizes, he fell from his horse three or four times, and was at last taken up by a neighbour and put to bed in a house on the road. He soon fell asleep; when, dreaming that he was falling into a furnace of boiling wort, it put him into so great an agony of fright that, struggling with all his might to call out for help, he actually did call out aloud, and recovered the use of his tongue that moment, as effectually as he ever had it in his life, without the least hoarseness or alteration in the old sound of his voice.'

*   *   *

Garden Warfare

And here are a few gardening tips, supplied by Samuel Cooke of Overton, near Marlborough, and published in about 1747 in a useful volume, the *Complete Gardener*. A contributor to *Wiltshire Notes and Queries* possessed a copy, and described it thus:

> The advice at the end of the work on general topics is certainly curious, and throws rather a lurid light on rural Wiltshire life of the time. After giving some instructions for the destruction or prevention of vermin, he says, sage and rue will keep toads from the garden; a lanthorn set on the side of the water will prevent the croaking of frogs; polecats and badgers, as also foxes, are numerous enough to require special traps for their destruction; bullfinches and gold-finches are to be exterminated; under 'bat-fowling, the manner of it', the author says, 'observe where these birds roost, as they do in shrubs, hedges, and trees'; mole-catching is a simple matter – put a head or two of garlick or onions in their holes, they will run out, as if frighted, and you may with a spear, or dog, take them; adders will fly from the smell of old burnt shoes in a garden.

*   *   *

Rooted to the Spot

Meanwhile, in a village a few miles away, none of these potent nostrums seems to have had any effect on the predicament of a certain Mr Dean. A very early (1724) press report tells the strange story:

> We hear from Collingbourn Kingston in Wiltshire that there is now living there one John Dean, who for three years past has been in one Posture, leaning in a Partition Wall between two Chambers; at first his head rested against the Wall, but by Degrees forc'd a Way through, as likewise for his shoulders, his Breast resting upon an Inter-joist; his Legs by long

standing begin to mortify, so that he cannot live much longer; he eats very hearty, and is always craving for Victuals; his Excrements are voided in the Place where he stands, which contributes very much to the Disagreeableness of the Object. Several People have endeavour'd to persuade him to move from the Place, but in vain, alledging that he cannot be easy in any other Posture, and if they go to use Violence, it puts him in a raving Madness; he sometimes talks very sensible, at other Times like a Lunatick, and believes that he is bewitch'd, which Opinion has prevail'd over the greatest Part of the Parish.

* * *

Wilkinson's Questionnaire

Forty years before the first issue appeared of the glorious ragbag of similar antiquarian culs-de-sac, *Wiltshire Notes and Queries*, a county society was formed at Devizes under the name 'Wiltshire Archaeological and Natural History Society', and this began to publish a magazine (as it still does). Folklore and folk customs made an appearance in the very first issue, and seem – very much to the society's credit – to have been regarded from the outset as an integral part of local history.

A leading enthusiast in the early years was John Wilkinson, who was rector of Broughton Gifford, near Melksham, from 1848 until his death in 1876. He was keen to encourage local clergy to write histories of their parishes to a common format, and he set out a detailed framework of 'heads of information' to be collected. Several, including his own on Broughton Gifford, were published, and some others remain in manuscript at the society's library. A detailed questionnaire was sent, on the bishop's authority, to each incumbent, and about seventy responded. Four of the questions concerned traditions and customs current in the parish at the time (the 1860s), and although most forms were left blank on this subject, there was a handful of replies. So far as I am aware, none has been published up to now:

Avebury: Mummers at Christmas. Eating cakes with honey and 'Lent-figs' on Silbury on Palm Sunday. Possibly an adaptation by the medieval church of some heathen custom to the act [account?] of the cursing the barren fig-tree on the Mount of Olives on the Monday in Holy Week.

Beechingstoke: It is said that one of the Raymonds of Puckshipton offered to rebuild the church if the lead of the roof was given to him. The parish accepted the offer and the church was rebuilt, and the roof covered with shingle tiles (1693). By this transaction Mr. Raymond is said to have netted a good sum of money. This must have been Charles Raymond who died in 1716.

Chilton Foliat: A loaf baked on Good Friday always remains good. And grated into clean water is a great cure for fevers, etc. Rain water caught on Holy Thursday is a cure for bad eyes.

Durrington: The only superstition which has come under my notice is that an aged woman nearer 90 than 80 told me –

perhaps five years ago – that she had gone out the night before and had shaken her apron to the moon, because no-one had given her any gift for some time, and that a present had come to her within a few hours.

Fittleton and Haxton: The people here think much of keeping Christmas, when some of the village youths come round, and act as 'Mummers'. They also speak of 'Tide Times'.

Heddington: When I first came here there was a very abominable custom of treating with rough music newly married couples. The boys and young men furnished themselves with old pots and pans, and amused themselves by beating them for half the night in front of the house. I believe the custom is now quite discontinued.

North Tidworth: I believe the common people 'blow away warts' to the moon. This they do for one another. I am not allowed to stand at the foot of the bed of a dying person as it hinders the departure of the spirit.

* * *

Oram's Grave

Presumably in the 1860s the rector of Heddington's attitude prevailed, that such superstitions were abominable. He seems, incidentally, to have witnessed a skimmington (a communal punishment for marital irregularity) and assumed that it was a wedding custom. By the 1890s, although fewer traditions would have survived, the questionnaire might have been more productive, since by then the study of folklore had become more respectable as a pastime for clergymen. Even the bishop took a personal interest, as this contribution to *Wiltshire Notes and Queries* reveals:

At the intersection of the old track from Salisbury to Warminster across the Downs, with that from Maddington to Codford

St Mary, on the boundary line of Maddington and Chitterne St Mary, is a barrow marked 'Oram's Grave' on the Ordnance 6in. Map. The Bishop, on his visit to us (23 March 1893), pointed out this name to me, of which I was previously ignorant, and suggested that it was the corruption of some British or Saxon name, which I doubted. Afterwards, on looking at the map, it occurred to me that as the grave was situated at the cross roads, Oram was probably the name of a suicide, buried there according to the old custom and law.

A conversation with widow Sarah Cook (aged 81) on 28 March 1893, proved that this was the case. She told me that in 1849 she and her husband were living in one of the Maddington Manor Down Barn Cottages, and in the other the shepherd lived, James White and his wife Elizabeth (formerly Windsor), a very good woman, aged 61, both of Chitterne. Elizabeth White told Sarah Cook that when she was a child she was coming home with her father from Salisbury (or elsewhere) and when they were near the crossways by the Clump, they saw many people coming from Chitterne to bury Oram in the barrow there, for he had hung himself with his own rope, and was to be buried there. Her father told her that 'her maunt be vraughten at what she saw for they wouldn't hurt she', and so she saw Oram buried. She did not tell Sarah Cook whether his body was in a coffin or not, but Sarah Cook thinks there was a coffin; certainly there was no parson and no service. The barrow has ever afterwards been called 'Oram's Grave', and the name is now perpetuated in the Ordnance Survey.

8 May 1893. – The Rev. A.C. Pinhorn, Vicar of Chitterne, told me the circumstances of Oram's burial are forgotten in Chitterne, except that the cause of his suicide was disappointment in love, and that a stake was driven through the body, which I think proves that though he may have been carried to the grave in a coffin, he was not buried in one. There is no record of the funeral in the Register, nor any charge for it in the parish accounts.

C l e r g y

Broughton Gifford

John Wilkinson's interest in folklore during the 1860s puts him ahead of his time, and must have seemed odd to many of his fellow clergy. But he had discovered from his own parish registers a kindred spirit in the person of one of his predecessors, a certain William Hickes, rector of Broughton Gifford from 1689 to 1733. 'We are most thankful to him,' wrote Wilkinson, 'he certainly provided for, if he did not anticipate, the demands of the parochial historian.' Near the end of his incumbency Hickes wrote the following note on a fly-leaf of his register:

In Novemb. Anno Dni. 1732. A house called the Church House, which had two chimnys, one at each end, was pulled down and the stones and timber used in the Rebuilding the House near the Parsonage House. (This House reached from the Lower Stile going to the Brook) to the Rails eastward as may from the Stoone wall left for Bounds of the Church Yard.

This Church House was Built by one Thomas Cookson, as appeared by a Stone in the outward Wall of the sd. house next the Churchyard Side, in which was Engraven a Pedlars Pack and on Each Side a Cock.

Some Poor people lived in it in the memory of a man who livd in the year Sixteen hund. eighty and nine and in particular (as I have been informd by some that could remember it) the Father of John Oatridge, which John Oatridge had a leg cut of and mended Shoos, in a house belonging to Esq. House in the lower end of the field near the Brook and was Buried in May 1703 which House was pulld down about year seventeen hundrd. and eleven or twelve.

About this Church House after it was pulld down were noises heard in the night like throwing the Timbers about one upon another and upon the Stones that Lay near by Mrs. Hunt and her two daughters that livd just by.

Likewise in the Farm House (lying by the Parson's House in wch. then livd one Robert Newman) while the Church house was Pulling down and after they heard the treading of one going up and down Stairs.

Also a Noise of throuing the Stones that were brought from the sd. Church House into their Barton, from one heap to another.

Over the years Hickes had many observations to make on the weaknesses of his flock. He was forthright in recording 'reputed' and 'pretended' wives, and 'illegal' marriages. One or two couples left things until the last moment:

John Tomkins of the paroish of Holt and Ester Stevens of the paroish of Broghton were maryed by licence. The man was about 65 years old, and was sick 3 or 4 weeks. The woman about 25 years. He scarce ever saw her till they came to Church to be married, nor spoke a word to her above his sign to mary her, but by another person, and it was agreed upon but the night before mariage, and were maried the next day, and he dyed the next day after mariage. So that the woman was a maid, wife, and widow within 24 hours, and supposed to be a maid as well as Widow and own'd to me she was a maid still.

Wilkinson, when he transcribed that entry for his history, coyly omitted the last observation, with the remark: 'The further revelations of the plain-spoken Rector concerning Mrs. Tomkins, do not admit of publication.' Why not, one wonders? But then one realizes that it is just one of many examples of the Victorians' knack of titillation, achieved by omitting an innocuous remark and then referring to it by innuendo. Of course the same code precluded any mention of another entry, by the next vicar, in 1735:

Jacob Bull married Miriam Bull, both of Broughton. The woman was delivered of a male child the same evening.

The moral tales which pepper Broughton's register are not only about matters sexual. Here is a sad story from Hickes about anger:

> Isaac Bull was buried, Aug. 13. He was thrown of his hors on Lansdown and dyed the next day. His mother he curs'd at his going out and she wish'd that he might break his leg or nec before he came home. He threw his mother downe and he mockt her, calling her snecking bitch and other reproachfull words.

No, we can't have that. Wilkinson omits the word 'bitch', and inserts three dots in its place. But when describing his own times Wilkinson is more candid and forthright. Here, in 1859, he describes housing conditions, marriages and amusements:

> The labouring population are very indifferently lodged. The cottages are abundant, but the dwelling rooms are few and small (the weavers devote the best lighted and largest apartments to their shops [i.e. workshops]), the sleeping accommodation is not such as to admit of the decent separation of ages and sexes. Wells are infrequent (notwithstanding the excellent water within a few feet of the surface), nor are the offices [privies] convenient or proper. The drainage is defective. This state of things is no more than might be expected in a parish, where the landed proprietors, being non-resident, want that interest in the people, which would naturally arise from personal communication. The poor here are not neighbours to the rich. In this respect we are no worse off than a large proportion of out of the way parishes, but we have disadvantages of our own. With hardly an exception, the cottages (originally for the most part encroachments on the commons) belong either to the poor occupiers themselves; or to proprietors, who are hardly removed from the labouring class; or to the farms, with which they are let. The

owners or the managers want either the means or the will (generally both) to promote domestic comfort. Though there are so many cottages and some vacant, yet rents are not low; three small rooms and 10 or 15 perches of garden ground fetch £4 a year. The explanation is, that a large proportion of the cottages for hire are owned by one person, who also keeps a beer shop and general store of such articles as the poor require. He works the rent against the shop, and the shop against the rent, so that he is able to keep up prices in both commodities.

St. Mary's Church, Broughton Gifford

The marriage ceremony is conducted about here in a manner which is not pleasing. It is a ceremony and no more. There are no pretty bridal customs, no strewing of flowers, no favours, no stocking or slipper-throwing, no nosegays.

That we retain the ring is owing to the requirement of the rubric, and we may thank the milliners for the artificial orange blossoms. Nobody comes to church, but the bride and bridegroom, walking down the street arm in arm, followed by one or two couples more, who are 'keeping company'. Parents never think of gracing the union with their presence...

The same remark applies to games and amusements; we have next to none. There were indeed, ten years since, the remains of a Michaelmas revel. Bushes were hung out at unlicensed houses, and the whole thing had degenerated into a mere drinking bout. The excise officers and the police extinguished it. Bull-baiting lingered here longer than elsewhere: there is a tradition of it on the common. So there is of cock-fighting: the pit is said to have been where the Rector's cucumber frame now stands. The moral odour of the place still hangs about it: the only thing he ever missed were five cucumbers stolen one Sunday morning. The chief village dissipation takes place at the Whit-sun meeting of the Benefit club. The neighbouring fair at Bradford Leigh used to be much frequented, and was generally accompanied by mischievous midnight revelry. This holiday gave a mnemonic date to 'the simple annals' of domestic life. I have heard old people reckon events, 'come next Bradford Leigh fair'. I have known a skimmington. A mob, with tongs, gridirons, saucepans, or anything they could get, surrounded the house of one who was said to be an unfaithful husband, and made most unmelodious music. Kattern cakes are carried about for sale on St Katherine's day, November 25th. It seems a pure matter of vulgar merchandise. There are no rhymes, no bowl, no jollity, no maidens making merry together and looking out for good husbands by help of the patroness of spinsters. We have no 'merry wakes, May games, and Christmas triumphs', of course no christening customs, but not even a harvest home. We are rather dull.

The 'we' is important. Wilkinson was one of that priceless band of clergymen who settled into their parishes and became totally bound up with the affairs of their parishioners. He was no detached observer, gone tomorrow, but an intimate historian.

He wrote his history as a model for others to emulate, and it is arranged according to the scheme which he had devised for parochial histories. His ideas were in turn derived from the *New Statistical Account of Scotland*, which had been compiled by local clergy.

* * *

A Temperate Vicar ...

But if Wilkinson failed to spur all his colleagues into producing copy for a comprehensive published history of Wiltshire, that did not mean that they were unwilling to chronicle their own parish events in private notebooks, for their own and their successors' reference.

John Augustus Lloyd was one such chronicler. His volume of parish notes begins in 1877, when he became vicar of Broad Hinton, high on the downs south of Swindon, and continues through the 1880s until his departure for Mere in November 1890. His successor, Vere Awdry, kept it going with rather less gusto for a few years, but then it gradually fell into abeyance.

Awdry's short incumbency was marred by tragedy. A widower, on 21st June 1891 he records that his little girl died suddenly of convulsions aged two years and one month, and was buried with her mother at North Bradley. For two months Awdry was absent from his parish on doctor's orders, but on 29th October he remarried, and brought his bride back to the village. They were, he reports:

> ... accorded a most hearty welcome by the villagers, the horse being taken out of the carriage, and the carriage with its occupants drawn into the vicarage grounds and up to the door by hand.

The following January the notebook records that:

... a small hand fire pump has been presented to the vicar for a wedding present. It stands in the vicarage hall always ready for use, and is at the service of all who need it.

A more protracted episode of parish history was chronicled by his predecessor. Lloyd was the son of a Bath magistrate and physician, and it was perhaps not surprising that he should espouse the cause of temperance. It was some eighteen months after his arrival that, in November 1878, he chaired a public meeting which inaugurated the Broad Hinton Church of England Temperance Society and Happy Home Union. Its minute book has survived, and shows that, as in the case of so many local initiatives, it was carried on with great enthusiasm for a few years, but then the regular meetings ceased. The last entry describes a public tea held in the village in May 1891, and attended by about 100. Lloyd had left the village by this date, and Awdry had taken over. The assistant diocesan secretary of the temperance society spoke – predictably – on the evil of drink and the dangers which might follow. His talk was preceded by a few half-hearted words of introduction from Awdry, who said that he had no experience himself but should be glad to hear concerning it.

But in Lloyd's time, when it was set up, the society had chalked up a famous victory. It was Lloyd's idea to revive the old patronal feast, held by the medieval church each year on the day of the saint to whom the church was dedicated. Broad Hinton's saint's day, St Peter ad Vincula, should have been on 1st August, but for temperance purposes the revived feast was held later in the month. The first festival took place on 18th August, 1879, and involved an afternoon service and sermon by a visiting rector, followed by a temperance tea and school feast. The minute book records that it was, 'quite a success', and includes a newspaper cutting which begins:

We have to record the success, in spite of some little difficulties, of the first annual festival of the village temperance society.

A fortnight later we learn what those 'little difficulties' might have been. Lloyd's parish notebook has an entry for 30th August:

> The licence of Henry Witt landlord of the Bell Inn in this village was taken away by the Marlborough bench of magistrates for being drunk and riotous on Sunday 17th instant. Broad Hinton Feast! How has a church festival degenerated and fallen through.

Sure enough, the *Marlborough Times* reports that:

> Henry Witt was charged with being drunk and disorderly at Broad Hinton, and fined 10/- and 18/6 costs.

His licence was not renewed, and the decision on its renewal was deferred.

Whether this was an isolated protest by the publican, or the result of an 'alternative' feast organized at the pub, we are not told. But there is an irony in the plight of Henry Witt. In reviving the patronal feast the vicar imagined that he was recreating a medieval church festival. What he forgot, or chose to ignore, was the alternative name for such events, the church-ale (because ale was brewed and consumed in great quantities in order to raise funds for the church fabric), and the fact that at the reformation such feasts were outlawed on account of the drunkenness and debauchery associated with them. It was Henry Witt who had revived the old tradition, and he might with more justification than the vicar, have exclaimed, 'How has the festival degenerated', when he discovered that only tea was being served at it.

But such was the Victorian perversion of ecclesiastical history. The temperance movement, having taken away the publican's livelihood, was now in the ascendant. In November 1880 Lloyd recorded in the parish notebook:

> The Bell Inn – Loveday having had possession for about one year became bankrupt, and John Austin a tee-totaller took it. He gave up 10th December finding it could not be made to pay honestly.

In January 1881 there is a note that it had changed hands again, and the census of April 1881 records that Henry Hopkins, a thirty-year-old carpenter and licensed victualler from Calne, was at the Bell; so it presumably reverted to being a conventional pub, as indeed it is today. But not to be outdone, the temperance society on 6th June 1881 opened its own alternative place of refreshment, a coffee tavern, in a cottage a few doors down the village street.

There were two classes of adult temperance society members, those who asserted that they were willing to do something towards the suppression of drunkenness, and those who were total abstainers. The latter signed the pledge:

I hereby agree, by God's help, to abstain from the use of intoxicating drinks, except at the Holy Communion, or under medical order, as long as I keep my card of membership.

At the inaugural meeting twelve joined in the former category, and six in the latter, but there were many new members, and not a few ignominious departures, during the first few years of the Broad Hinton society's existence.

From the vicar's point of view there was one most satisfactory convert to the temperance cause, and this warranted a special entry in the parish notebook:

Dec.10th 1879. The Rev.J. Campbell gave a temperance lecture at the schoolroom. Henry Witt late of the Bell Inn signed the pledge, which he has not yet broken (Nov.1880); he is quite altered for the better.

Lloyd kept up the momentum. In June 1880 he presided at a temperance meeting, by reading extracts from the *Temperance Chronicle* and afterwards the humorous piece, 'How to cook a husband'. Then in August preparations were under way for the second annual feast. This too proved to be a bittersweet experience, as the parish notebook records:

Monday 16th Aug.1880. Temperance festival and tea service at 3 pm. Rev.J. Campbell preached. Day fine and numbers present large. The late landlord of the Bell Inn kept a stall for the sale of non-intoxicating drinks in the vicarage field. As if to counter-balance this one of the members of the fete committee who had previously broken his pledge very brutally beat his wife the day previous.

This was not the first lapse. As early as 16th April 1879 the minute book records:

The name of Charles Pickett was removed, he having declined to try to keep the pledge for the future, offering no apology to the society for the disgrace cast upon it, and neither communicating with the president nor returning his card.

But we are not told what that disgrace was, and there is probably no way of ever finding out. The last of the regular entries in the minute book also has an intriguing aspect. It refers to a meeting on Boxing Day, 1884.

A very enjoyable evening was spent – the proceeds just covered the expenses, including some unfortunate accidental breakages.

*   *   *

...And an Intemperate Curate

Not all clergymen, however, were so concerned to promote good living and counter the evils of drink. Henry Hunt, the radical demagogue, recalled the brief career of a curate of Enford (near Pewsey) at the end of the eighteenth century:

The Sunday arrived, and my father, as the principal person in the village, always anxious to be the first to shew his attention to a stranger, and particularly when that stranger was clothed in the dress of Pastor of the parish, waited upon him at the Inn or Pot-House, where he had taken up his quarters, and not only invited him to dine, but also offered him a bed and a stall for his horse till he was better provided at the Vicarage. I, of course, accompanied my father, and we had little difficulty in getting over the first introduction. He was a young man of easy manners and address, and without the least ceremony, accepted the invitation to dine, etc; but he informed us, that he had made a bargain, and had taken lodgings and intended to board, with the landlady at the Swan, as he could not bear the thoughts of living in a dull country Vicarage House by himself.

We went to Church, where he dashed through the service in double quick time, and 'tipped us', as he had previously informed me he would, a *Rattling Sermon*, as a specimen of his style of oratory. He appeared a clever thoughtless youth, of twenty-five; but the rake, as my father said, 'stood confessed in his eye', and its effects sat visible upon his brow. After dinner he took his wine like a *Parson*, and before he had finished a bottle he was as drunk as a *Lord*; so much so, that he was utterly incapable of performing the afternoon duty without exposing his situation to the whole congregation. My father was shocked at his indiscretion, and sent a hasty excuse to put off the afternoon service... I took the hopeful and reverend young gentleman, who had been so recently inspired by the Holy Ghost to take priest's orders, a walk into the fields, to recover him a little, as my father thought him a very improper guest to introduce into the drawing-room to his daughters. In the course of our walk he professed a very sincere and warm friendship for me, and promised himself a world of pleasure in my society; and he frankly and unblushingly informed me, that he had brought with him from Oxford a bad venereal complaint, which, he added, was most unfortunate, as he was fearful that he should inoculate all the pretty damsels belonging to his new flock, which would be a *cursed Bore*...

He lived but a short time; having soon fallen a victim to his profligate course of life. He was little more than a year, I think, the Pastor of the Parish, and he administered the sacrament, and performed all the other offices of the Curate, when the effects of his drinking did not interfere with it, and during this time he always lodged at the public house. This was a sad example for the people of the parish!

L i f e ' s R i c h T a p e s t r y

Great Native Stamen

Clerical irregularities have always been a fertile source of prurient gossip, and we shall stumble across another instance (from Keevil, this time) later on. But if vicars were capable of the occasional over-indulgence, that was as nothing compared with some of their parishioners. Here is an obituary notice:

EXTRAORDINARY POWERS: The late Mr Joshua Dixon, of Downton, in this county, who in 1801 died suddenly at the age of 103, had all his life been a remarkably free-liver. According to his own calculation he had consumed two thousand gallons of brandy, without taking into account a variety of other kinds of liquor. He moreover enjoyed his faculties to the last. He was twice married, and of his numerous offspring by both wives, the oldest had died at the age of 70, while the youngest was only 18 at the father's death. Had this man practised the temperance of some patriarchs he might probably have attained the age of 150. The question is a difficult one. He doubtless lived longer as an habitual drinker, than he could have done as an immoderate feeder. The two seldom go together. The very strong men live on in spite of everything. It will be an interesting spectacle to see (as doubtless the world will yet see) to what amount of longevity, great native stamen will conduct the strictly temperate and virtuous man.

But then perhaps, as the old joke runs, the virtuous man would not actually live longer – it would just seem longer. And in any case I am not sure that we should trust the calculations of a man who claimed to have drunk two thousand gallons of

brandy, however enjoyable his faculties. Here is another eccentric
– an eighteenth-century aristocrat this time – out and about
enjoying himself:

> Bampfylde Moore Carew [the son of a Devon rector, who
> adopted the lifestyle of a gipsy and wrote books], disguised
> as a shipwrecked sailor, on nearing Longleat fell in with
> another in the same plight as himself; after having been
> successful in obtaining alms and food at the mansion, they
> adjourned to a public house, and, having had a good carouse,
> separated.
>   Shortly afterwards Carew was overtaken by two horse-
> men sent by Lord Weymouth to bring back the two sailors.
> When ushered into the great man's presence Carew was
> treated very roughly. He was then removed to await the
> capture of his comrade, and soon that ragged gentleman
> entered the room where Carew was confined. They had just
> time for a hurried consultation together before they were
> again separated, and Carew was once more brought before
> the Lord of Longleat, who thereupon, to the unbounded
> astonishment of the prisoner, disclosed the extraordinary
> fact that his ragged shipwrecked comrade was none other
> than himself! It seems that he was in the habit of thus
> playing the vagabond, partly to relieve a natural ennui, and
> partly to learn what was really going on in the neighbour-
> hood of his vast estates. I should add that he insisted on
> Carew staying with him at Longleat some time.

It would be interesting to know the name of Lord Weymouth's 'local'. The most appropriate would perhaps have been an
establishment recorded at Monkton Deverill, a few miles from
Longleat. In August 1877 members of the Wiltshire Archaeological
Society, meeting at Warminster Town Hall, were treated to a
lecture on 'Some account of the tavern signs of Wiltshire and their
origin', by our old friend the Rev. Alfred Smith (who seemed to
be able to turn his hand to anything). The subject generated
considerable interest, and there seem to have been a number of
contributions from the floor of the meeting, which were included

as footnotes when the paper was subsequently published. But that was not the end of it:

> On the day following that on which this paper was read before the Society, at Warminster, the archaeologists, in the excursion to Stourhead, halted at Monkton Deverill, and here it was discovered that the village hostelry, now denominated the 'New Inn', was once designated by the far less commonplace, if somewhat eccentric sign of 'The Tippling Philosopher'!

I came across this reference some years ago, and subsequently discovered that there had been an inn of the same name in London. Still it seemed odd to find it in such an out-of-the-way place as Monkton Deverill. I wondered, in fact, whether someone had been pulling the archaeologists' collective leg. But then one day I found in the Wiltshire Record Office that the alehousekeepers' recognizances for the Warminster area in 1751 include, most unusually, the sign of the house as well as the name of the licensee. And there, at Monkton Deverill, was 'The Tippling Philosopher'.

Our next eccentric also haunted the Warminster area, and probably could have regaled us with a fund of stories about tippling philosophers. But she fell on hard times, as this newspaper obituary from about 1777 tells us:

> Lately died at Bishopstrow, her native place, near Warminster, in Wilts, the celebrated Juliana Popjoy, in the 67th year of her age. In her youth, being very handsome and genteel, she was taken notice of by the late celebrated Beau Nash, a gentleman noted for his gallantry, dress, and generosity; when he soon prevailed on her to tread the flowery paths of pleasure with him, she was accordingly ushered into the blaze of the world, was mounted on a fine horse, and had a servant to attend her. This seemingly happy state continued some years; but at last, Mr Nash's finances being low, a separation took place, when poor Juliana experienced a sad reverse of fortune, and was driven to almost the lowest ebb of misery. However, she did not, like too many of her

sisterhood, take to parading the streets for a livelihood, but to a very uncommon way of life. Her principal residence she took up in a large hollow tree, now standing within a mile of Warminster, on a lock of straw, resolving never more to lie on a bed; and she was as good as her word; for she made that tree her habitation for between thirty and forty years, unless when she made her short peregrinations to Bath, Bristol, and the gentlemen's houses adjacent; and she then lay in some barn or outhouse. In the summer time she went a simpling, and occasionally carried messages. At last, worn out with age and inquietude, she determined to die in the house where she was born; accordingly, a day before her exit, she reached the destined habitation, where she laid herself on some straw, and finished her mortal pilgrimage.

* * *

Death's Rich Tapestry

Of course, the pithiest obituaries are to be found on tombstones, and witty epitaphs have been collected and copied for centuries. Charles Dickens, who during the 1850s published a magazine, *Household Words*, was responsible for popularizing this one, which he attributed to Pewsey. It still turns up, incidentally, in present-day anthologies.

> Here lies the body of Lady O'Looney, Great
> Niece of Burke. Commonly called the sub-
> lime. She was bland, passionate and deeply
> religious, also she painted in water colours
> and sent several pictures to the Exhibition.
> She was first cousin to Lady Jones, and of
> such is the Kingdom of Heaven.

One consequence of its publication was that the rector of Pewsey at the time, Thomas Ravenshaw, was, as he put it, 'much worried by incessant applications for "correct copies". The fuss, one imagines, soon died down, but Ravenshaw continued to be interested in the subject, and in 1878 he published a collection under the title, *Antiente Epitaphes*. There is a presentation copy in pristine condition in the Library of the Wiltshire Archaeological and Natural History Society at Devizes. In an appendix to his book he finally laid the ghost of Lady O'Looney, who had never been at Pewsey at all, and showed up Dickens (or whoever Dickens had copied it from) as guilty of considerable poetic licence.

The original, in fact, relates to a Mrs Jane Molony, who died in January 1839 and was interred in St George's Burying Ground, Hanover Square, London. Her epitaph runs to 483 words, and describes in confusing and tedious detail the estimable achievements of most of her relatives. For the record she was not 'bland, passionate and deeply religious' at all, but 'hot, passionate and tender, and a highly accomplished lady...'. How she came to be linked with Pewsey is not explained.

Ravenshaw's book prints epitaphs from all over England, and includes many medieval examples. But here are two from eighteenth-century Wiltshire. The first, from his own church at Pewsey, is rather touching; the second, from Potterne, is facetious:

> SAMUEL AUSTIN
> Stay awhile and spend a tear
> Upon the dust that slumbers here
> And while thou readst the fate of me
> Think on the glasse that runs for thee.
>
> MARY wife of the above
> I grieve to think I cannot grieve no more
> To think my dearest Friend is gone before
> But since it pleased God to part us here
> In Heaven I hope to meet my dearest dear

> Here lyes MARY the wife of JOHN FORD,
> We hope her soule is gone to the LORD;
> But if for Hell she has chang'd this life,
> She had better be there than be John Ford's wife

Ravenshaw's successor, Bertrand Bouverie, wrote A *Few Facts Concerning the Parish of Pewsey*, which was published in 1890. It is probably the worst local history of a Wiltshire parish published around that time – or should that distinction go to *A Sentimental and Practical Guide to Amesbury and Stonehenge* by Lady Antrobus? Anyway, despite Bouverie's imperfections he does include an anecdote and an epitaph recorded in a letter sent to him in 1885:

Upon one of my visits we were told that there were three men drinking together at the Phoenix, who were named respectively – Deadman, Coffin, and Ghost. The last was a pedlar, who used to carry about silks and haberdashery; who the other two were I forget.

Sometime before – about 1815 perhaps, or earlier – there had died a certain Mr E—— in Pewsey, upon whom was written an epitaph, the author of which was not known, and I forget the name of the subject, but I have heard him spoken of as a most unhappy, fretful man. There was a schoolmaster in the village, a Mr Strong, who may perhaps have written them. He conducted the singing in the church, and was, though rather pedagoguish and pompous in manner, a clever man and a very good teacher:–

Here lies, to rest for evermore,
A body ne'er at rest before;
To an early grave untimely sent
By physic, wife, and discontent;
The oddest mortal, while alive,
That Nature ever could contrive;

Where he is gone is hard to say,
And we will hope the better way;
If soar'd above, 'tis ten to four
He's tired of Heaven in an hour:
If down to hell, the devil grim
Will quickly be as tired of him.

And here, to round off our little collection of epitaphs, is another, also first published during the 1890s:

Among the combatants on the Parliament's side at Edgehill was a Wiltshireman who afterwards attained celebrity by extraordinary longevity. This was William Hiseland (Hazeland?), born in the year 1620 during James the First's reign, and dying in 1732, in the reign of George II. He commenced his military career at the early age of 13, probably in the Earl of Pembroke's militia; he fought his way all the way through the Civil Wars, and was with William of Orange's army in Ireland, and closed his foreign services in the Flanders campaign under the renowned Duke of Marlborough. Either in active duty or as an invalid he bore arms for the extraordinary period of eighty years. The Duke of Richmond and Sir Robert Walpole, in consideration of his long services, each allowed him a crown a week for some time before his death. The old man helped himself in another way, having had three wives in the course of his life; his last marriage was contracted the year before his death, viz. 9th August, 1731. A picture of him taken at the age of 110 is said to be still extant. His epitaph, given below, is on his tombstone in the burial-ground of Chelsea Hospital:

Here rests WILLIAM HISELAND,
A veteran if ever soldier was;
Who merited well a pension
If long services be a merit:
Having served upwards of the days of man.
Antient, but not superannuated,
Engaged in a series of wars
Civil as well as foreign;
Yet not maimed or worn out by neither.
His complexion was florid and fresh,
His health hale and hearty,
His memory exact and ready.
In stature he excelled the military size;
In strength surpassed the prime of youth.
And what made his age still more patriarchal;
When above one hundred years old,
He took unto him a wife.
Read – fellow soldiers, and reflect
That there is a spiritual warfare
As well as a warfare temporal.

Born 6 August, 1620
Died 7 February, 1732, aged 112

This remarkable career was noted by a Devizes antiquary, James Waylen, to whom we shall be further indebted when we delve into crime and punishment.

*   *   *

More Ham – less Calf

Waylen was interested in collecting examples of longevity in Wiltshire, and he also pasted into his scrapbook oddments on all kinds of related subjects. Here is an undated piece of anthropological nonsense:

Peculiarity in Wiltshire Men – I have noticed that in Wiltshire, as in some other counties west of London, the men have no calves to their legs. All of them, young and old, wear knee-breeches, and a sort of tight leather legging, and this exhibits more palpably their thin shanks. Otherwise they are generally handsome men, mostly a middling size, thin and wiry. I was told by a gentleman, who seems to know the rural population of England well, that in all the counties where bacon is eaten as a staple article of diet, the men have small calves. I cannot see any reason for this: but whether it be bacon, or whether it be that a bacon-eating race have invaded these counties, and have brought a peculiar formation of legs with them, it is a fact that they have calveless legs, no matter how well fed or how starving they may be. The jolly-faced farmers have the same kind of legs as the lean labourer. – Adam Brown.

Calfless Wiltshireman approaching Devil's Den , Clatford, near Marlborough

Dabchicks, Gudgeons and Dogs

What a strange thing to write to the newspaper about! But this kind of attempt to categorize inhabitants of an area by physical or mental characteristics has a long history. John Aubrey's thoughts on the differences between the peoples of north and south Wiltshire, which are included in his introduction to *The Natural History of Wiltshire*, are too well-known to bear repeating here. Another manifestation of such interests is the coining of nicknames, and some of these in the middle ages turned into family surnames which are still in use today. 'Fulljames', for example, derives from French *fol jamb*, or 'bad leg', 'Pettigrew' is *petit cru*, 'small growth', 'Smallbone' and 'Armstrong' are self-explanatory.

At a more local level nicknames have often been applied by one community to a rival one, usually in derision. An excellent example, supplied in Ida Gandy's book, *The Heart of a Village*, is Ramsbury people's nickname for their neighbours at Aldbourne – 'dabchicks'. A dabchick, apparently, arrived one day on Aldbourne village pond, to the great mystification of the villagers, who had never seen one and could not identify it. Their ignorance amused the Ramsbury folk, who watched dabchicks every day diving in the River Kennet, and so they taunted anyone from Aldbourne by shouting 'dabchick' after them. This association, Mrs Gandy points out, became respectable, and was commemorated by a dabchick emblem engraved on bells cast at Aldbourne before 1757. It is, therefore, a sobriquet of long standing.

Along the Wiltshire-Somerset border disdain for one's neighbours was expressed in a little ditty:

> *Trowbridge knobs,*
> *Bradford gudgeons,*
> *Hilperton tiedowns,*
> *Bradley donkeys,*
> *Road waspies,*
> *Beckiton bees,*
> *Frome dumbledories, and*
> *Warminster fleas.*

This was collected by a lady from Purton, Ethel Richardson, who also preserved a rhyme along similar lines about the church bells in the villages around Shrewton:

Shrewton brave bells,
Ma'anton ting tang,
Rollestone frying pan,
Upper Ar'ston besom stick;
Lower Ar'ston candlestick.
Stoke slats,
Barwick strails,
Stubbleford rats,
Without any tails.

Notice, incidentally, the dialect forms of Maddington, Orcheston and Stapleford.

Deeper still into the heart of Salisbury Plain, here is one more nickname, the subject of an enquiry to *Wiltshire Notes and Queries* in 1896.

I have heard it said that there is nothing which upsets a native of Imber so much as the sobriquet of Bungey, or Bungay, and that they obtained the nickname by roasting a dog so named. Can anyone supply me with further information as to this?

Lock up at Bradford on Avon,
surmounted by gudgeon

Nobody replied.

But while on the subject of dogs, let us end this chapter with a touching story of canine loyalty. It is recorded in the diary of Captain William Owen, of Glansevern in mid-Wales, who was travelling home through Wiltshire in December 1751:

The 13th in the morning walked from Heytesbury to Warminster, and stayed there the remainder of the day. One Jacob Dunn, that kept the Packhorse Inn, gave me a little dog, of the Dutch-mastiff breed, which I took with me into Wales, and left with my mother. After her death in August 1754, it accompanied my niece, Molly Owen, to her father's at Tanycoed, where she kept it for her grandmother's sake. When I returned into the country after an absence of ten years, this dog was grown decrepit, grey, and blind with old age. Upon my entering the house it ran with the utmost fury and open-mouthed at me, as I thought to seize me by one of my legs, but upon coming up to me, stopping, suddenly jumped up and fawned upon me, and it was with difficulty I could prevent its following me wherever I went.

C r i m e ...

The darker side of Cherhill

Notebooks, diaries, and minute books, of course, later become the stuff of the village historian. Here the skilful author of an exhaustive history of his village, James Blackford of Cherhill, near Calne, is turning his attention to the life of crime. Three paragraphs are taken from local hearsay, but the fourth is supplied by the notes of a former rector, William Plenderleath, who served the parish from 1860 until 1891:

> Many years ago one of the Cherhill farmers noticed his stack of firewood was disappearing but was unable to find out where it was going. One day he took a piece of wood from the stack, cut three holes in it and then filled it with gunpowder, afterwards rubbing dirt over it to cover the marks. He then replaced the piece of wood in the stack. A few days later the piece of wood was missing; shortly after the report went round the village that a cooking pot had been mysteriously blown off the fire at a house in Greens Lane. The farmer then knew where his wood was going.
>
> Many are the tales told about the large elm trees which used to line the main road at Cherhill. One of them stood near the Bush Inn and wagoners used to draw their teams of horses and wagons under this tree whilst partaking of refreshments inside the inn. If the old inhabitants' tales are correct, many are the sides of bacon, sacks of corn and cheeses that have been lifted off wagons by ropes manipulated by men up in the tree. On one occasion a side of bacon was missed; next day persons were surprised to see a stick lying on top of the chimney of a thatched cottage at the bottom of Labour-in-Vain Hill. Someone in authority became

curious and wanted to know why it was there. The replies not being very satisfactory he decided to investigate; the missing side of bacon was discovered hanging up the chimney by a rope attached to the stick.

On another occasion two men wanted a cheese. It was decided that No. 1 should go in and entertain the carter while No. 2 moved a cheese from the wagon to a safe hiding-place known to both. Having completed his task No. 2 returned to the inn to help entertain the carter. After a little while No. 1 left the inn for a few moments and removed the cheese from its hiding-place to another known only to himself. After the carter had gone both men went to divide the cheese, but it had disappeared. Little did No. 2 suspect that No. 1 had moved it to another place so that he could retain it himself.

My own uncle, [wrote Plenderleath] who was born in 1776, when he heard of my having accepted a living in Wiltshire, solemnly exhorted me never to think of driving across the downs without my servant and myself being provided with firearms. There was also a band of footpads known as the 'Cherhill Gang' who relieved many a traveller of the pence which he had intended to pay his scores owing at the Bell or the Black Horse. Two old men who were said to have been members of this Society lived on into the period of my residence, and anyone noticing their venerable white heads bowed over their big prayer-books would have taken them for very Village Patriarchs thus ending their simple and blameless lives. One of these men is reported to have sometimes gone out upon his marauding expeditions in the summer time without a stitch of clothing, as he said that not only did such an apparition frighten people on a dark night, but also that a naked man was less easily recognised than one who appeared in the ordinary costume of the period.

Yes, I suppose so, but it must have been rather difficult to conceal the stolen goods.

In fact, having written that remark, I now find that Plenderleath had pondered the same problem. In a piece entitled 'Cherhill Gleanings', which he published in 1889, he included a version of

Section from Greenwood's map of Wiltshire, 1820

the same story, and ended it thus:

> The usage must, however, I should think, have entailed some
> practical inconveniences with regard to the disposal of booty
> if trade was brisk; and also, if the victims did happen to show
> fight, it would have been apt to hurt!

And then, for good measure, he recounts another anecdote:

> I remember a story that our late neighbour, Mr Henry
> Merewether, was very fond of telling of how he was returning
> one dark night from Devizes, where he had been defending
> a man charged with highway robbery. So clearly had he
> shown the jury that, notwithstanding the existence of
> suspicious circumstances, his client was a man whom it was
> impossible for one moment to suppose capable of such a
> crime, that the latter was triumphantly acquitted, and left
> the dock, as the newspapers say, 'without a stain upon his
> character'. But the same night, alas! on the top of the downs,
> Mr. Merewether was himself requested to stand and deliver.
> And, still more sad to relate, the author of this request was
> his maligned client of the same morning! Those of us who
> remember Mr. Merewether will feel sure that the tale must
> have ended happily, and that whether by reason of his strong
> right arm or his persuasive tongue – (I think, if I remember
> rightly, it was the former) – he came off triumphantly, scot
> free.

*　　　*　　　*

Mine Host

But if, unlike Mr. Merewether, you had not the stature to defend
yourself, a journey across the Cherhill Downs on a dark night in
the eighteenth century must have been a nerve-racking experience,
and the comforting light of the Black Horse Inn a welcome relief.
Why, incidentally, is it called the Black Horse, when it stands
beneath the Cherhill White Horse cut on the hillside? And why,

for that matter, is the perfect place to watch the sun set over West Wiltshire the garden of the Rising Sun at Bowden Hill? No matter. The point is, that the cheery inn meant safety and good fellowship.

The Black Horse Inn opposite the Cherhill White Horse

Or did it... Here is a newspaper report from January 1842:

About three weeks since a perfect male skeleton was discovered in a field attached to a brickyard, in the chapelry of Stert, a short distance from Devizes. It was within two and a half feet of the surface of the field, and was found by a young man, whilst digging for clay; and who, attaching very little importance to the circumstance, took the bones up, and in the course of the day reinterred them. The fact, however, having been communicated to some of the clergymen of the neighbourhood; and those clergymen having been previously informed that murders had been committed near the spot, and that within a few years other skeletons had been dug up in the same field, felt very anxious to obtain any information that could throw light on the affair; they therefore caused the bones to be disinterred, and sent for Mr Whitmarsh, the Coroner, who held an inquest on them at the Bell Inn, Lydeway, on Monday last, when several aged persons were in attendance to give evidence...

It appears that about eighty or ninety years ago, there was a public house called 'The Shepherd and his Dog, kept by Thomas Burry, near the three mile stone on the Salisbury road; that Burry himself was of ill-repute, and his house of worse; that at that period large numbers of pedlars travelled the road; that many of them sought shelter at the Shepherd and Dog, but that few left the house alive, or if they did, it was only to be murdered on the road, and that the road then ran near the brick field. An old man named Sutton, of Urchfont, 88 years of age, recollects when he was a shepherd boy, threescore and ten years ago, that a person named Withers, whilst drinking at the house, overheard some persons concerting the murder of a Scotch pedlar then there, and that Withers went to Urchfont, and gave information of the fact, when the Urchfont people came and rescued the pedlar through the window. The cry of 'Murder', this old man said, was then very frequent in the neighbourhood of the Shepherd and Dog; and he has known several persons dug out of the brick field. There is also a tradition that when old Burry died, the bell would not sound, and that there were such noises as had never before been heard. The license was afterwards withdrawn from the house. A person named Edwards, said he knew an old man named Mower, a smuggler, and a friend of Burry's, and that sometime before his death, he heard him say that he had killed many a man between the Charlton Cat and Wedhampton, and buried them at Wroughton Folly. Edwards also said that when he was a boy, persons used to be afraid to pass the corner at the Shepherd and Dog. The owner of the brick field said that some years ago he discovered a skeleton in the same field, and from its position, it was evident that it had been pressed by force into a hole not large enough to contain it; and that a twelvemonth ago another skeleton was dug up.

A descendant of Burry's – an old man verging upon fourscore years – was also examined, but nothing could be elicited from him, farther than that he was not answerable for what other people did. He was repeatedly asked whether there was not a trap door to the cellar, and whether he himself had not very recently filled the cellar with gravel, but he evaded the question, and would give no direct answer. He lives in the very house that was the Shepherd and Dog.

W.D. Barker, esq., surgeon of Devizes, examined the skeleton, and said he had no doubt, from the size of the thigh bones, that it was that of a male person. On the top of the skull there was a perforation, which must have been effected by some sharp instrument, and which was sufficient to cause death. In his opinion this perforation was made prior to interment, and the person of whom the skeleton was the remains came to his death by violent means. The jury therefore returned a verdict to that effect.

*　*　*

To Bournemouth for Tea

Smugglers and highwaymen have acquired a romantic image, even to the extent that the exploit of the 'moonrakers' – cunning brandy smugglers – has become the symbol of Wiltshire one-upmanship, and a matter of local pride. In reality smuggling was a nasty, shadowy business which is seldom well-documented. But Wiltshiremen were certainly involved, as a tombstone at Kinson (now a Bournemouth suburb) darkly commemorates:

> To the Memory of Robert Trotman late of Rowd in the County of Wilts, who was barbarously murdered on the Shore near Poole the 24 March 1760.
>
> A little Tea one leaf I did not steal
> For Guiltless Blood shed I to God appeal
> Put Tea in one scale human blood in t'other
> And think what tis to slay thy harmless brother.

The tradition, it was said, was that he was a smuggler, and met with his death in an affray with the coastguard.

More Problems on the Road

Of Wiltshire highwaymen there is a great deal more evidence, thanks largely to the Devizes antiquary of the nineteenth century, James Waylen. He kept a scrapbook (now in the Wiltshire Archaeological and Natural History Society's Library) into which he pasted newspaper cuttings about highway robbery, and anything else that took his fancy. In 1856 he wrote a series of articles for the *Wiltshire Independent*, and these were subsequently published, anonymously, in book form. The Stert inquest, printed above, comes from his scrapbook, as does the following short account, which illustrates one misfortune for the gentlemen of the road which had not occurred to me before. There you lurk by the roadside, black cape, loaded blunderbuss, curious hat – 'Stand and deliver', you cry,... But no-one answers:

> Wednesday evening three coaches were stopt between Devizes and Marlborough, by two highwaymen. There being no passengers in the two first, they desired the coachmen to lend them a shilling each, for they were quite broke down, and they would pay them well for it another night. From the third coach they took about six pounds.

That little episode probably dates from 1782. Six years earlier, prompted by news of an archaeological excavation at Silbury Hill, a correspondent to the *Salisbury Journal* sent in a story about a less violent, but more subtle, form of highway robbery – daylight robbery might be a better description:

To the Printer of the Salisbury Journal:
SIR. As the attention of such gentlemen as have a taste for antiquities is, I imagine, at present fixed on what passes in digging Silbury Hill; I thought that the following anecdote, which was told me long ago by one who was a party in the transaction, might serve to amuse the antiquarians till their workmen at Silbury had finished their search; and if you can find room for it in your paper, 'tis at your service...

A poor boy was carrying a pitcher of milk along the road near Silbury-hill, and unluckily fell down and broke the pitcher; a taylor, who lived at Abury [Avebury], just by, met the boy crying for the loss of his pitcher and his milk; and at that instant a coach came in sight. The taylor, who was a man of humour, bid the boy be comforted, and told him he would try to get something for him of the gentry in the coach, and for this purpose bid him cry out lustily as the coach was going by. The coachman was, as was expected, ordered to stop on hearing the boy's cries, and the people in the coach enquired what was the cause of the boy's lamentations; the taylor stepped to the coach side, and told them that the boy had reason to lament, for that he was carrying home an urn which his father had just dug out of one of the barrows; that as a piece of antiquity it was of great value; that Dr Davis, of Devizes, who was known to be a great antiquarian, would have given a guinea for it, etc. This excited the curiosity of the gentry in the coach to examine the broken pitcher, and thinking that the pieces might be joined together, they offered to give a crown for it, which was accepted: the taylor gave the boy a shilling to make good his loss, and put the remainder in his pocket. The gentry in the coach drove away with the broken pitcher, supposed now to be a Roman urn, and probably is now shewn in the musaeum of some antiquarian as such, and much admired by the Virtuosi. WILTONIENSIS.

But Dr Davis (remember him from chapter one?) was not to be fooled so easily. He was presumably the source of the story.

Another rather unusual traffic incident occurred some fifty years later:

In July, 1829, Sir Goldsworthy Gurney made his famous journey in a steam carriage from London to Bath and back. Gurney was a surgeon in Marylebone, greatly given to the working out of inventions in his spare time, and it took him some years to complete his first 'motor' in his back yard in Albany Street. He accomplished the journey to and from Bath at the rate of fifteen miles an hour, and there was only one disturbing incident, when a crowd assembled at Melksham set upon the machine, and having burnt their fingers, threw stones and seriously wounded the stoker.

Gurney's Steam Carriage

Rising again

Well, maybe that was just a touch of xenophobia, or an understandably hostile reaction to alarming new technology. But when it came to thieving, that was a different matter. Nothing was sacred, as this story from Purton illustrates:

It is surely well to impress upon the young the spirit of reverence, and that the Church and God's Acre which surrounds it are hallowed ground. In the old days this was unhappily not the custom, for we are told that when any parishioner wanted a good flat stone, he repaired to the graveyard to pick out one which might suit his purpose. It is even said that someone in Purton wanting a new bottom for his oven upon which to bake his bread pressed a tombstone into the service, and when the bread was duly baked, plainly upon the bottom of the large loaf could be read the words, 'Here lies the body of...'.

When a story is considered particularly good there is always the danger that oral transmission and improvement will not be sufficient. It will be turned into a poem. Is this a rustic equivalent of the Homeric epics, which were couched in verse as an aide-memoire to the bard? Or is it the less remote legacy of the ballad seller? 'The Village Baker', as reported by Ethel Richardson, Purton's historian, extends to 63 lines, but we shall join the action at the point where the baker is showing the parish mason, whom he had employed to mend the oven with tombstones, the result of his handiwork:

> He took him to the bakehouse,
>   Where a curious sight was seen,
> The words on every loaf were marked
>   That had on tombstone been,
> One quartern had 'in memory of'
>   Another 'here to pine',
> The third 'departed from this life
>   At the age of ninety-nine'.

A batch of rolls when they were done
Had on the bottom plain,
The trusting words distinctly marked
'In hopes to rise again,'
A batch of penny loaves came next
Which said 'our time is past,
Thus day by day, we've pined away,
And come to this at last.'

*   *   *

A Poet who lost his head

Stealing tombstones is bad enough, but the Trowbridge historian can cap that story. The town's most famous rector was the poet George Crabbe, who is best remembered now for the tale of Peter Grimes. Crabbe died in 1832, and a monument was erected to his memory in Trowbridge parish church, where he was buried. Fifteen years later, in 1847, repairs to the church were necessary, and his grave was disturbed. It was then that his skull disappeared; and a mystery remained over its whereabouts for the next thirty years. The *Trowbridge Advertiser* takes up the story in 1876:

Strangers are inclined to question the correctness of the story of the lost skull, but as we have had it from the lips of the gentleman who has been the means of restoring it, we give it:- Thirty years ago, I was standing by the open vault of the Poet Crabbe, with the then Rector of Trowbridge, the late Rev.J.D. Hastings. The church was then undergoing thorough alterations, and the floor of the chancel was up, for the purpose of lowering it. The removal of the surface disclosed the vault of the Poet Crabbe, where he was buried fifteen years before. It was his wish to be buried in a plain coffin, hence the rapidity of decay... The workmen tossed up a skull, and Mr. Hastings said, 'That is the skull of Poet Crabbe; this is where he was buried'. I was a student of phrenology then, and said, incidentally, 'I should like to take a cast of that skull'. Nothing more was said, and we left.

George Crabbe

That evening a dirt-begrimed labourer presented himself at the side door of my father's house and enquired for me, saying in a sepulchral voice, 'I've got it'. 'Got what?' I said. 'Old Pa'son Crabbe's skull! and we should like a drop o' beer on the job, please Sir.' 'I don't want it; I can't have it; put it back; don't let my father see you here with it; where is it?' I said. The man replied, 'I put it in my tommy-bag when you was gone, as I heard you say you should like to take a cast, and now I can't put it back again, for the floor is all rammed down and cemented, and the stones laid, and if you don't have it I shall destroy it, that's all', and he was proceeding to tie up his 'tommy-bag', and to depart to fulfil his threat. To save the skull from such a fate, brought about by the simple remark I had made at the graveside, I decided to take care of it, and carried it indoors, but my father would not have it there, so I tied it up in a silk pocket-handkerchief, and hid it in a dry place for seven years, when I removed it to my iron chest, and there it has been ever since. I offered it to the late Rector for re-interment, but there was no opportunity for raising the chancel floor... I have shown it to the poet's son, before he went to Australia, and have since, at his request, forwarded him photographs of it in four different positions.

In 1876 the skull was placed in a polished oak box, and re-buried near Crabbe's vault in the chancel of Trowbridge parish church.

...And Punishment

A Gruesome Business

Justice seen to be done had a rather more literal connotation when public executions took place at or near the place where the crime was committed. The hanging of William Jaques for murder at Stanton St Quinton in 1764 was one of many such awful warnings which lingered on years after the event. John Britton, a Wiltshire antiquary who made his name in London and wrote his autobiography, was not born until seven years after the hanging, but he knew all about it nevertheless:

> An event connected with this locality, and noticeable, as illustrating the superstitious opinions which prevailed amongst nearly the whole population of the time, may be narrated; as the relation of it made an indelible impression on my young mind, and indeed impressed me with the belief that the phenomena of lightning, thunder, and storm always accompanied human executions. When a boy, I often passed a gibbet, in Stanton field, on which a man had been hung in chains for murdering a negro in Stanton Park, a large wood so called. The two had been seen together at Malmesbury, and at the village of Stanton, and the murderer was noticed on the same day by some of the inhabitants of Kington, walking at a quick pace through that village inquiring his way to Chippenham. He had killed his companion, rifled his pockets, and was on his road to Bristol. Within an hour after the murder was committed, the body was discovered by a woodman, who communicated the intelligence to the inhabitants of a neighbouring farm: a hue-and-cry was raised, the man was traced through Kington, and arrested at Chippenham on the same day. He was

John Britton

conveyed to Salisbury, tried, and condemned to be hung. According to my father, who often repeated the tale (one story forms a staple article for retailing in a country village, for a long space of time), he, with almost all the inhabitants of Kington and the neighbouring villages, went to see the murderer hanged on Stanton Common. As the culprit approached the place, a small black cloud was observed over the gibbet: it increased, and at the time of the execution had extended over a wide space. When the man was 'turned off', there was a vivid flash of lightning, with thunder, and a violent storm arose, and continued during the remainder of the day.

*   *   *

More Hanging About

Britton, no tittle-tattler, was quite right about the potency of such stories. They passed into folk memory and endured centuries of retelling. In the burial register for Maddington (which is now part of Shrewton on Salisbury Plain) an entry reads:

William Lawne, sonne of Giles Lawne, barbarously slaine neere the Windemill, Sept. 23rd, and buryed the 24th of the same, 1666.

In September 1900, 234 years later, a contributor to *Wiltshire Notes & Queries* was able to fill in the details:

Canon Lowther informed me that the old clerk of Orcheston St George, whom he found in office when he took the Rectory in 1830, told him that the man who was murdered at the Gibbet, had taken a large sum of money at Warminster market. The ostler of the inn where he put up knew this, and after he had left Warminster followed him, and shot him at the place where the Gibbet now stands, making off with the money. The murderer was apprehended, and hanged in chains at the crossways of the London and Warminster, and

Shrewton and Devizes tracks. Old people remembered the stump of the Gibbet when I came to Maddington, and there is still a tradition that where it stood, 'on a place like a grave (which I could never find) nothing will grow'. Canon Lowther told me that the story was stated to him by the clerk in Orcheston St George churchyard, who pointed out a place to him, saying, 'And here, sir, lies the man that heard the shot fired'. The Canon had no idea that it took place so long ago as the entry in Maddington Register Book proves it did, and he believed that the clerk claimed to have known the man who heard the shot fired.

*　　*　　*

Incident at Watkins' Corner

It is in the nature of anecdotes and oral traditions, such as these examples, that they are improved each time they are given an airing. The parish historian uses them for light relief, but must learn to spot a tall story when he or she finds one. Ethel Richardson, the historian of Purton, near Swindon, amassed a fine collection (including the token thunderstorm) when she looked into the origin of Watkins' Corner:

> One of the last horrible gatherings of this kind took place in the year 1817, at a corner on the high road between Purton and Purton Stoke, when people flocked from Gloucestershire and distant parts of Wiltshire to see John Watkins hanged. He had been convicted of a murder, no paltry theft this time, he had killed Stephen Rodway of Cricklade, and so well deserved to suffer.
>
> A small boy, aged but seven years, son of the Vicar of Purton was there, and in charge of his father's gardener, who, horrible to relate, held the child up, so that he should get 'a better view'. This fact was told to the author by the daughter of this boy, quite 100 years later.
>
> Many stories are still remembered in connection with this particular hanging. The church bells were tolled as the

murderer was taken past Purton Church to where the scaffold had been erected, and a small prayer book, still to be seen at Purton, was placed in his hands, from whence to read the 108th Psalm, beginning, 'Awake up my glory, awake lute and harp'; the concluding verses, 'Oh help us against the enemy for vain is the help of man', were truly more suitable to so dread an occasion. Souvenir hunting, it is said that the murderer's collar, boots and braces were eagerly seized by spectators, and carefully preserved to show to friends for many a long day afterwards. Gruesome too were some awful stories told later. It was said that one night two men were drinking at the inn at Stoke, and that one bet the other he would not dare to crawl down a ditch near Watkin's Corner, and say, 'Well, Watkins, how are you feeling?' The man took up the bet and went; crept into the drain and asked the question. The other, unknown to him, had placed himself within reach in the darkness, and replied promptly, 'Very cold and miserable'. This reply so alarmed the first man, that, having a weak heart, he promptly died of fright. Then people say that the hangman, on his way home that day, was thrown from the trap, and broke his neck; while a fearful thunderstorm raging, seemed a protest from the sky, but which certainly may have frightened the horse, and so upset the cart! Further, years later, the very shed at Blunsdon where the gallows were stored, caught fire, and consumed them to ashes. So poor Watkins became more famous in his end than he had been in life; for the corner is always known by his name, and the story of his end told to strangers.

* * *

A *Final Twist*

Victorian journalists were perhaps more cautious about checking their sources, but they were never coy about crime and punishment, as they were about sins of the flesh. Frederick Large was a Swindon journalist who worked on the same paper, the *North Wilts Her-*

ald, and in the same office, as he tells us, for 54 years 9 months (think on that!). In 1931 he published a volume of reminiscences, and from it this sad little story will, I think, bear repeating:

> I remember a case in which a burglar had been apprehended for an extensive robbery of jewellery in Wood Street. Some remarkable facts were brought to light in this case. The culprit, who was of most gentlemanly appearance, with a long frock coat and high silk hat, had made himself acquainted with a Post Office official, the Post Office being immediately opposite the jeweller's premises. By this means he became acquainted with the habits and customs of the jeweller, and noticed that he was in the habit of visiting the Postmaster most evenings for friendly intercourse. Watching the jeweller leave the shop on one of these visits, the thief seized his opportunity to enter the premises and take away a large quantity of jewellery, to the value of several hundred pounds.
>
> Shortly after this the Post Office official, who had become friendly with the criminal, fell upon evil ways, with the result that he was committed to a long term of imprisonment. During his incarceration he supplied information to the prison authorities which enabled them to trace and bring the jewellery thief to justice. The ex-Post Office official, clad in convict's clothing, was brought to give evidence, with the result that the prisoner was committed to the Assizes, where he received a sentence of 14 years penal servitude. As a result of turning Queen's evidence, the ex-Post Office man's sentence was reduced from five years to three, this being the closing chapter of a most sensational case, which caused much excitement in the whole district. Strange to say, on the day in which the ex-Post Office official was released from Portland, he fell down some steps and broke his leg. He was taken back to his quarters and the broken limb was set, but the injury turned to mortification, and proved fatal. He was buried in a convict's grave.

Fiendish Devices

It was a subject which appealed also to the Victorian antiquaries, who sometimes appear to have taken a slightly unhealthy interest in ancient modes of punishment. The very first issue of the *Wiltshire Archaeological and Natural History Magazine* has an article about the cucking stool (ducking stool or tumbrel) at Wootton Bassett. Its author, Frederick Carrington of Ogbourne St George, near Marlborough, drew on his legal background and contacts to collect parallels from other parts of England, and so explain this unpleasant device. He included a description by a French lawyer, which was first published in English in 1715:

Cucking Stool – the way of punishing scolding women is pleasant enough. They fasten an arm chair to the end of two beams, twelve or fifteen foot long, and parallel to each other, so that these two pieces of wood with their two ends embrace the chair which hangs between them on a sort of axle, by which means it plays freely, and always remains in the natural horizontal position in which a chair should be that a person may sit conveniently in it, whether you raise it or let it down. They set up a post, upon the bank of a pond or river, and over this post they lay almost in equilibrio the two pieces of wood, at one end of which the chair hangs just over the water; they place the woman in this chair, and so plunge her into the water, as often as the sentence directs, in order to cool her immoderate heat.

Coming round for more

A few years later Carrington contributed a much longer paper to the magazine, entitled 'Facts and observations as to the ancient state of Marlborough'. That indeed describes the first fifteen pages of his article, but then he warms to his subject, and the remaining twenty-nine pages are given over to hanging; the pillory; whipping the poor; the cuckingstool; and the brank, or scold's bridle. A lively and good-humoured speaker, by all accounts, such was his enthusiasm that he took along his own brank, a nasty piece of restraining headgear for scolding women, to display to his audience when he delivered the paper. He would certainly have been interested in the following contribution to *Wiltshire Notes and Queries* which appeared some thirty years after his death:

> In a copy of the *Statistics of Crime in Wiltshire*, 'formerly belonging to Mr Alexander, for many years the Governor of the Gaol at Devizes, and previously the Keeper of the Bridewell at Marlborough', a sentence is recorded at the Wilts General Assizes, 1807, against a man named Benjamin James, of two years' imprisonment, and to be twice exposed in the pillory. In a marginal note Mr Alexander writes:
>
> 'This man was confined in the Bridewell, and stood in the Pillory at Marlborough, once at the commencement and once at the expiration of his sentence. The mob, by whom the sentence of the law was inflicted, was very merciful to him on the first occasion, and the man was foolish enough to say that he would stand another such a punishment for a pot of beer, which was not forgotten when the time came for him to undergo the second operation. Preparations were made by the people a long time beforehand. Rotten eggs, dead cats, cabbage-stumps, and everything that could be thought of, was plentifully prepared, and he received a most dreadful punishment. A cabbage-stump was thrown at him which stuck in his cheek, and the machine went round several times with the stump sticking in his face. When released he presented a most horrible spectacle, and his life was despaired of a long time.'

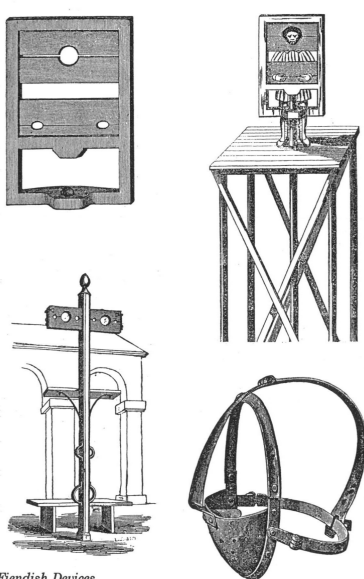

Fiendish Devices
Top: Marlborough Pillory with and without victim
Bottom left: Whipping Post
Bottom right: Brank

The pillory was a machine which kept revolving, the prisoner was fastened to the upright pole, and the populace pelted him for one hour with anything except stones or other hard substances.

*   *   *

A *Barbarous Villain*

Occasionally, in spite of whatever punishment was dictated by the law, public opinion regarded a crime as so heinous as to brook no mercy. Here is an example reported in the *Gentleman's Magazine*:

Feb.25th 1764: Henry Timbrell, a petty farmer, near Malmesbury, in Wilts, was committed to Salisbury gaol for castrating two lads whom he had undertaken to breed up for a small sum. These unhappy youths the barbarous villain had before endeavoured to destroy by throwing them in the way of the smallpox; but not succeeding, his rapacity at length suggested to him this operation, by which he thought to qualify them for singers, and to dispose of them at a good price. They are both alive, and their wounds healed. For this fact he was tried at Salisbury assizes, found guilty of a misdemeanour, the Coventry Act not reaching his case, as lying in wait could not be proved against him; his sentence was four years imprisonment, a fine of 26s. 8d., and to find security for his good behaviour during life. The sentence was thought so unequal to his crime that it was with the utmost difficulty he was preserved from the rage of the populace.

*   *   *

Salisbury Water Torture

On other occasions, especially when the offence had not affected them, and was not perceived as a threat to society in general, people might take a more detached view, and look on with amusement. Here is a newspaper cutting collected by James Waylen. It dates from about 1780:

Thursday last we were entertained with a trial of an uncommon kind, at a military tribunal under our Council House in the Market Place. – Two of the dragoons now quartered in this city had been guilty of petty thefts or frauds on their comrades, and instead of a court-martial, the officers left the conviction and punishment of this trivial offence to the men. Accordingly they were drawn up; one of them, dressed as formal as a judge, with a knapsack round his head, came escorted by a guard, took his seat in an elbow chair, with his clerk attending to take minutes – the two culprits brought by a file of musqueteers – a jury of twelve, collected indifferently from the men, and a charge given – the evidence then heard, and on conviction the Judge, with great solemnity, after observing on the evil of their offences to their society, sentenced them to undergo the punishment of booting and bottleing, and which was inflicted immediately, by each juryman giving a dozen blows with a jackboot on the posteriors of the criminal, and then pouring bottles of cold water thro' the sleves of his coat, the arms being extended, which produced something equivalent to the fit of an ague, from the trickling of cold water down his sides.

*   *   *

A *Courtroom Drama*

This, of course, was child's play for the reporter. But when we start to browse among the late Victorian broadsheets we encounter columns – whole pages sometimes – devoted to individual trials. It is probably not generally known that the first published book (really little more than a booklet) by the Wiltshire naturalist, novelist and 'prose-poet of the countryside', Richard Jefferies, was a practical manual for journalists. *Reporting, editing and authorship: practical hints for beginners in literature,* was published in 1873, and displays some of its author's frustration with his lot as a reporter, as well as his aspirations for a literary career. It deserves closer scrutiny from devotees of Jefferies than it has so far received.

But I am digressing. Jefferies gives detailed instructions to the cub reporter about how to cover a trial – how to organize his papers, what pen to use, who to approach for details of names and charges, all the practical details which his own experience had taught him. Later on in his booklet, however, he tackles the broader issues:

The principal rule in editing a paper is to insist upon every line being readable. The public want no solid cleverness, no prosy compilations, however good in their object, they require amusement. Men will read an 'Extraordinary Discovery in California' who would contemptuously pass over long speeches and dull leaders. With the vast flow of news that now comes in there is a constantly increasing impatience of long accounts – a constant tendency to condense everything.

During the first half of 1881 readers of local newspapers in Wiltshire had to contend with lengthy accounts of two trials, and public interest was maintained because of the salacious nature of the accusations, and the 'fresh revelations' (as modern tabloids would regard them) which kept coming to light. The first was a libel case brought by the vicar of Keevil (near Trowbridge) against a fellow clergyman, arising out of allegations that he had misconducted himself with various parishioners. The second was described by the *Wiltshire Times* as 'the fracas between noblemen'. Lord Edward Thynne brought a charge of assault against three men who had accosted him while driving his pony carriage between Laverstock and Salisbury. We soon discover that there was more to it than that. But the best Victorian journalists whet our appetites not with vulgar headlines; instead we are treated to sparkling dialogue, apparently reported verbatim, though in reality carefully edited and selected for dramatic effect:

Did you not know at the time that it was the Marquis Townshend who struck you? – No.

If you had known it was Lord Townshend you would not have been astonished at it? – Yes I should.

I am sorry, but I am bound to ask you this question: 'Were you not in 1872 a constant visitor at his house, enjoying his hospitality?' – Not hospitality. I was frequently in his house, but not to see him.

Mr.Powning [counsel for Lord Edward] protested against questions being asked relating to events that occurred nine years ago. He advised his lordship not to answer any further questions relating to the subject.

A legal argument ensued, the result being that the Bench ruled that the questions were admissible either in extenuation or aggravation of the assault.

Mr.Tatlock [barrister for Marquis Townshend]: You were a constant visitor at Lord Townshend's house in 1872? – Yes.

And you eloped with his wife? – Yes.

Have you, from that time to the day of the alleged assault, ever met Lord Townshend face to face? – Never.

Did you ever get a beating from Lord Macduff? – I was assaulted by two men, one of whom was Lord Macduff.

In consequence of this same affair? – Yes.

That was the *Wiltshire Times* reporting the first hearing of the case in May 1881. When it came up before Quarter Sessions at Warminster in late June the facts were rehearsed once more, and on this occasion the *Salisbury Times* reporter showed that he too could write dialogue worthy of Oscar Wilde:

You, I believe, saw Lord Townshend some years ago? – Yes.

I think, in those times, he had the pleasure of receiving visits from you at his house in Dover-street? – Yes.

What year was that in, Lord Edward? – In 1872.

How long did those visits last? – From the beginning of 1872 till November.

Then, I believe, it was in 1872 you were kind enough to take his wife away from him? – It was (laughter).

At this time you were married – and I am not going to say anything further about a lady now dead? – Yes.

Before you took her away did you write her several letters asking her to go? – I don't recollect whether I did or not.

Will you be pleased to tell us? – I can't recollect; I might have done.

You can't recollect! Did your wife unfortunately find one of them – do you remember that? – Yes.

And she sent it up to him? – Yes.

Mr.Swayne [the presiding magistrate]: I don't think this is necessary.

Mr.Tatlock: Sir – on this point I shall not say another word. (To Witness) When you took her away from Lord Townshend's did you meet her in a cab in the street going to see her sister? – No.

That is false? – It is untrue.

Did you take her from Dover-street? – No.

Will you mind being kind enough to tell me where you took her from? — I don't see what that has got to do with the assault ('Oh, oh,' and laughter).

Mr.Tatlock: But I am going to ask you (laughter).

And so it continues, column inch after column inch. And at the end of it all Lord Edward won his case, at the expense of losing all vestige of self-respect in a blaze of humiliating publicity. And we are left suspecting that greater issues and darker secrets remain to be discovered.

This, of course, is the stuff of the novelist and the playwright. Hence the progression of Richard Jefferies' thought: reporting – editing – authorship. And in the following year, 1874, he published his first novel..

N e w s p r i n t

Unexpected Arrivals

'Every line being readable', was Jefferies' stricture to newspaper-men. Sometimes the news was, almost literally, heaven-sent, as the editor of the *Swindon Advertiser* was pleased to discover in May, 1869:

About two o'clock on Friday morning last, as P.S. [Police Sergeant] Stephens was standing in Taunton-street, New Swindon, he was startled by a very brilliant white light overhead. On looking up he saw a globe of perfectly white fire apparently about a foot in diameter descending towards him. When it came within about one hundred yards of him, it suddenly turned red throwing out a number of sparks like a rocket. It continued red until it came within about thirty yards of the ground and then turned green; finally disappearing when about fifteen yards from the earth and apparently in the middle of the street. The light was so brilliant that everything around was distinctly seen, and the sudden change to darkness produced a very peculiar effect. He went to the spot where the fire appeared to fall but could find nothing.

But wait, I think that I may be able to help him with his enquiries. I seem to remember reading in a footnote somewhere – yes, here it is, in a book on early motoring:

The first road traffic signal in this country appears to have been a semaphore erected in Westminster in 1868. It had red and green lamps lit by gas. Its short life terminated abruptly in a violent explosion.

I wonder whether the explosion could have been so violent as to propel the apparatus to Swindon. I suppose that we shall never know.

Swindon was not the only place in Wiltshire where things fell out of the sky. In July 1892 another 'unidentified flying object' landed near Devizes:

Fall of a balloon at Bulkington.– The aeronauts missing.– A large balloon with a car attached passed over Devizes about 7 o'clock on Tuesday morning, and shortly after came down in a field at Bulkington. A young farmer named William Hillier, who was mowing grass, narrowly escaped having his horses struck by the car, which passed directly over him, only a few yards high. It next struck the hedge, and bounding up for about twenty feet, descended two fields off. He at once made for the spot, and found men running from all directions. After first securing the balloon to a tree, he made a survey of the car, but found in it nothing but a card and a clasp knife opened, which had evidently been used to sever the ropes as one was cut through, and another gashed in several places. The car, which smelt of seawater, had at the bottom of it a quantity of shingles and small shells, and had apparently been dragged along the sea shore, besides being dipped in the sea. There was also nearly half an inch of snow in the car when first discovered, showing that it must have mounted to some high altitude before descending. The car also bore the appearance of having been dragged on rocks, as it was grazed and one or two ropes torn off. The inscription on the card was:—'L. Demeyer, 96 Rue de l'Ourcq, 96, Paris, Membre d'Academie, d'Aerostation

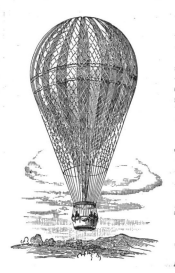

Meteorologie, et Fabricant de Vannerie en tous genre.' P.C.
Osmonde was soon on the scene, and with the aid of several
helpers the gas was allowed to escape, and the balloon was
packed in a cart and taken under his care.

For the newspaper editor this story had the additional spice
that, when he went to press, the mystery remained unresolved.
His readers had to wait until the following week to discover that
the outcome was happy, and that the three French 'aeronauts' were
safe and well.

Fillers

In fact, there is a good deal of news in Victorian local newspapers
which leaves us crying out for more. The weekly paper did not carry
only local news. National and international events were also
carried, sometimes of audacious triviality. Here, for example, is
a one-liner from the *Wiltshire Times* in August 1881.

> For throwing cayenne pepper at Oldham a woman has been
> fined £5 and costs.

But you cannot leave it there, with us readers in suspense.
Why did she throw cayenne pepper at Oldham? Did she have a
grudge against the town? From where did she throw it? How much
did she use? Did she hit Oldham, and if so what was the effect?
Was anybody hurt? Was £5 the usual fine for throwing cayenne
pepper, or was it considered lenient or excessive? Were the costs
for clearing up the pepper?

I suppose that it just goes to prove what we all know, that
a little cayenne pepper goes a long way!

–Ah, now that is the kind of joke that our Victorian newspaper
readers would definitely have enjoyed. It would have appealed to
their sense of humour.

Indeed, when, as often happened, there were not enough
readable local and national news items and advertisements to fill
the Procrustean bed of an eight-page broadsheet, the editor would
resort to a column of puns and clever remarks, headed 'Wit and

Humour' or 'Facetiae'. Here are some examples, supplied by the *Trowbridge Chronicle* to its readers in 1879:

Coming to the point – Sharpening a pencil.

Most people are like eggs – too full of themselves to hold anything else.

What is the difference between a poor gun and a masquerade costume? –º One is fired and doesn't hit, and the other is hired and doesn't fit.

Nothing is so fatal to the romance of a kiss as to have your girl sneeze at the very climax of osculation.

A great many men are of the opinion that a certain quantity of wine is good for a man. It is the uncertain quantity that hurts him.

An unsuccessful vocalist went to a country poor-house, and delighted the inmates with his singing. He said it was a natural thing for him to do, as he'd been singing to poor houses ever since he began his career.

'With all thy false I love thee still,' murmured a young man as he calmly handed his girl the artificial teeth that she had sneezed into his lap.

Satisfied at last – A contented shoemaker.

First irate female: 'I'd hate to be in your shoes.' Second ditto: 'You could not get into them.'

A new nation seems to be rising in Europe – consternation.

A young couple were returning from the theatre, where they had witnessed a love scene acted. 'I can do better than that myself,' the young man remarked. – 'Why don't you, then?' she replied.

Well, I don't know about you, but Victorian jokes never did much for me – except for the last one, but I think that 'love scene' meant something rather different in 1879. And what is this obsession with sneezing while snogging (oops, sorry – osculation)? Is it some kind of omen, as the Romans believed, or has it something to do with the lines from the nursery rhyme, 'Sneeze on Tuesday, kiss a stranger... Sneeze on Saturday, see your sweetheart tomorrow'? Or are we still in Oldham?

Another device for filling space and amusing readers which was occasionally tried was the riddle. The crossword puzzle in its present form is a twentieth-century invention, but here, as early as 1775, a contributor came close to using the cryptic clues beloved of crossword compilers:

ENIGMATICAL LIST OF TOWNS AND VILLAGES IN WILTSHIRE:

1. Half a large fish, a vowel, a consonant; two-fifths of a celebrated orator, and two-thirds of a grain.

2. Three-sevenths of a bigot, a vowel, the last letter in the alphabet, and two-sixths of respect.

3. Half a noted perfumer, three-fourths of an aromatic herb, and four-eighths of a bird.

4. Three-fifths of an infant, a consonant, what is used in writing, and a much-esteemed dish.

5. Half a useful firing, half an amphibious creature, a weight, three-fourths of treacherous, and what the sun does.

6. Four-fifths of a character in the Irish widow, and a passable river.

7. Two-thirds of a domestic animal, the initial of a tender passion, a liquid letter, and a vowel.

8. Half a large bird, two-fifths of a wedge of gold, and a title of distinction in Spain.

9. Half an excursion, a consonant, and what we do with the dead.

10. Not low, and merit.

11. Five-sevenths of an insect, a youth, and a vowel.

12. Three-fifths of a month, a liquid letter, and what a member of parliament represents, will make known the native place of-

NANCY I———s.

Now you may need a little help with that. If I tell you that there was an eighteenth century London perfumer by the name of Richard Warren & Co.; and that *The Irish Widow*, a play of 1772 by David Garrick, features a character called Martha Brady – you should not have too many problems. Mind you, there seems to be a mistake in clue 3 — for 'starling' read 'sterling'.

*　　*　　*

A Whiff of the Orient

If to our way of thinking the Victorians were not very successful when they were trying to be funny, when they were in earnest their quest for self-improvement through knowledge has a certain piquancy. Here, for example, is another filler from an 1879 *Trowbridge Chronicle* which caught my eye:

IN THE HAREM. When a Turk has disposed of his visitors he goes into his haremlik to dine or breakfast, first removing his babouches. This custom of removing one's shoes before entering a room is not a religious superstition, but comes of the necessity for keeping carpets clean, seeing that they

fulfil the purpose of chairs, tables, sofas, in other countries.
The bedroom of a harem may be furnished like Parisian
boudoirs: but custom is stronger than fashion, and Turks
of both sexes like to recline or sit cross-legged on the floor.
Their carpets are curiously soft and thick, and the carpets
over the doors shut out all draughts and noises. Through
the open windows that look out on the garden come a scent
of roses and the hum of bees, mingled with the laughter of
children, who are playing on a well-trimmed lawn, under
the eyes of the dark-eyed Circassian nurses. The mistress
of the harem — the Buiuk-Hanum (great lady, to give her
full title) — dresses much like an English lady nowadays,
reads French novels and plays the piano, though she dons
upon state occasions, such as the chalvas, when she enter-
tains other ladies. Chalva means a cake, but has come to
designate a party at which that dainty is eaten, just as we
say tea for tea-party in England. When a Turkish lady gives
a chalva, her husband is perforce excluded from the harem
while the strange women are in the house. These guests
begin to arrive towards six, accompanied by their maid-
servants and negroes carrying lanterns, and bringing their
children with them. Closely muffled, they divest themselves
of their burnouses and babouches in an ante-room, and put
on delicate slippers, which they have brought with them in
bags. The reception-rooms are brilliantly lighted up with
pink wax-candles and scented with fragrant pastilles. There
is no kissing or hand-shaking between the hostess and her
guests; but each lady, as she comes in, lifts her hand grace-
fully to her heart, her lips, and her brow, which means, 'I
am devoted to you with heart, mouth, and mind'. This mode
of salutation, when smilingly performed, is very pretty. The
greetings being ended, the company seat themselves on
chairs if there be any Frank ladies present; if not, they betake
themselves to the divans and carpets, and the cake-eating
begins.

I am sure that it must come as a great relief to all my right-
minded readers to learn that this – and not what they thought

– was the kind of excess that went on in a harem. Indeed, after reading that reassuring note respectable parents in Victorian Trowbridge need have had no more qualms about allowing their daughters to visit Turkey, than they might about them attending a Wesleyan tea meeting – unless, that is, too much cake was considered bad for their complexions. I wonder whether any Trowbridge girls ever did end up in a sultan's caravanserai.

*　　*　　*

The Rustic Polymath

Reading some of these fillers, one cannot escape the conclusion that the editor has made them up during his lunch break. Here is a dubious piece, originally published in the *New London Magazine* long before most local newspapers had begun, in May 1786:

The following is an exact copy of a sign, hung out at a village in Wiltshire:

ISAAC FAC TOTUM, barber, perr-wig maker, surgeon, parish clerke, scool mester, blacksmith, and man-midwife.

Shaves for a penne, cuts hare for toopence, and oyled and powdered into the bargin. Young ladys genteely edicated; lamps lited by the hear or quarter. Young gentlemen also taut their grammor langwage in the neetest manner, and great cear takin of their morels and spelin. Also salme singin, and horce shewine by the real maker. Likewise makes and mends all sorts of butes and shoes, teches the ho! boy [hautbois or oboe] and Jews harp, cuts corns, bledes and blesters on the lowest terms. — Glisters and purges at a penny a piece; cow-tillion and other dances taut at home and abroade. Also deals holesale and retail perfumerry in all it's branches. Sells all sorts stationry wair, together with blackin balls, red herrins, ginger bred, and coles, scrubbin brushes, treycle, mouce traps, and other sweetmetes. Likewise Godfrey's cordiel, rutes, potatoes, sassages, and other gardin stuffe.

N.B. I teaches joggrafy, and them outlandish kind of things. A bawl on Wensdays and Frydays; all performed (God willin) by me, ISAAC FAC TOTUM.

*   *   *

The Man in the Moon

Another way in which an editor, short of copy, could fill out his paper was by running a kind of gossip column, obliquely poking fun at people and places under the cloak of anonymity. Nowadays such 'in-jokes' of a century or more ago generally fall flat, either because the innuendoes have been lost, or because of the changing taste in humour which I noticed earlier. But here are a few of the better contributions (all from 1883) to a column which ran during the 1880s in the *Trowbridge Chronicle*. The supposed correspon-

dent was none other than the 'Man in the Moon', who was able
to look down bemusedly on the Trowbridge area, and pry into all
sorts of personal goings-on. This conceit was maintained to the
extent of poking fun at an amateur astronomer who, he alleged,
was prying back again:

What is it on the move in Chapmanslade that makes every
man so watchful of his neighbour's interest, as for each to
be a detective of the other's acts? A man has been too free
at Christmas, gets fined for it at Warminster, and a few days
afterwards he is summoned before the Westbury bench to
answer the same charge for the same offence, on the same
day, in the same street. It seems that one side of Chapmanslade street is in Warminster magisterial division, and the
other side in Westbury division. The offender seems to have
imbibed on one side too freely and afterwards, in that state,
crossed to the other side, and this is said to have constituted
the double offence. The magistrates very wisely refrained
from punishing the man twice for one and the same offence.
It shows how watchful the Chapmanslade folks are of each
other's welfare.

Valentine's Day, that annual outlet for spite and spleen
of the most reprehensible kind, was again characterized in
Trowbridge – I hope not elsewhere – by the faithful postmen
seen labouring along bearing most curious missives. What
connection a dip candle, a wooden monkey on a stick, a box
of cockroaches, and other tender trifles have to do with St
Valentine, I leave your readers to judge. The spiteful and
splenetic senders, moved by the most pitiable of motives,
somehow or other do it so clumsily that they cannot conceal
their animosity; for postmarks and clumsy attempts to
mystify handwriting are sometimes eloquent.

What is the meaning of sending candle-ends as valen-
tines? I am told the piece of dip candle that has been sent
from one to another around this town, through the post, each
one mistaking the right party who sent it. How much farther
it will go is not known. Perhaps a vigorous blow from the
P.O. stamper will flatten it out of all semblance, and termi-

nate its career.

The parties who, the other night, carried off some choice rhubarb from a garden in Waterworks Road, can, I am informed, have a valuable recipe how to preserve it, on calling at the owner's residence.

*   *   *

More Trivia

Nothing, it seems, was too inconsequential or too remote to be printed in the local newspaper when there was space to fill. Following the Oldham pepper scoop the *Wiltshire Times* continued through the silly season of 1881 with more information which the good people of west Wiltshire had previously done without:

The electric light has been introduced into the smoking room of the Junior Carlton Club.

According to an Arkansas paper, an intoxicating spring, whose waters taste like apple brandy, has been discovered in that State. A Missouri journal notices the statement, and sarcastically adds that Nature knows where her gifts will be best appreciated.

On Tuesday, as a Birmingham auctioneer, Mr. Fellows, was conducting a sale at Garrison-lane, Birmingham, and was saying 'Going, going, gone' previous to knocking down some articles, the floor gave way, and precipitated a number of persons, including several brokers and women, some with children in their arms, into the cellar beneath. Several of the people were hurt.

Luminous paint is being used for country post boxes in Cambridgeshire, so that they may be seen in the dark.

The stamp duty of 3d a pack on playing cards amounted in the last financial year to the net sum of £14,652.15s.9d.

Yes, I know what you're thinking. Actually, that comes to 1,172,223 packs of playing cards – perhaps more, as the figure was net. No television, you see, and nothing much in the newspaper.

F a i r s

Selling a Wife

Journalism is a hurly-burly world, and the scramble to meet a deadline can lead to tawdry prose. Richard Jefferies was aware of the pressures:

> The editor should never argue. He will have twenty people, of twenty different minds, to see him on a market-day, all bursting with their own ideas. Physical exhaustion would be the result of an attempt to convince them, besides every one would be offended. His object is to acquire information, he has merely to listen, and to put forward no view, except to help the speaker to a better comprehension of his own ideas.

But later there would be time for reflection. We have already been introduced to Master William Morris, who went 'In Search after Ozone and Oblivion' (what a modern ring that title has!). He was the founder of the *Swindon Advertiser*, in 1854, and he remained its editor until his death in 1891. He had plenty of opportunity to pick up unusual stories during his career. This one will have a familiar ring to readers of Thomas Hardy, as it foreshadows the action at Weyhill Fair upon which the plot of The Mayor of Casterbridge hinges. Morris published the following in 1885 – serialization of Hardy's novel in *The Graphic* began in January 1886:

> Among the poor, however, in some parts of the country at least, there existed a tradition that a man might rid himself of a faithless spouse in an equally legal but far less expensive manner – by putting a halter round her neck and

leading her by it from the home to the public market place, and there publicly disposing of her by auction. The parties to whom I have referred not only believed in this tradition, but they made all the necessary arrangements for taking practical advantage of it. The halter was bought, such notice as was considered necessary of the intended sale was given, and the day and hour fixed when the sale was to take place in the Swindon Square or Market-place. It was, of course, also arranged that the young navvy was to be there and to become the purchaser, for the sum, I believe, of sixpence and a pot of beer. At this time, no doubt, there was a very general impression on the minds of the ignorant and unlettered that such a sale of a wife as that contemplated was legal, and that the liability to maintain her was thereby transferred from the vendor to the purchaser. For some reason, which I never heard, the sale did not take place, although there was a large gathering of persons in the Square at the time appointed to witness it. Although at this time the school-master had not come in, the policeman had, and I have always entertained a grave suspicion that it was through his interference that so many persons were deprived of the sight they went out to see, and the town spared the disgrace of having a woman led into the public square with a halter round her neck for public sale.

*　　*　　*

Salisbury Fair

When there was plenty of time and too many column inches to fill, the reporter might indulge himself in what may best be described as a little essay. Here is a cutting of 1892, anonymous but not without literary skill, and quite satisfying in its balance of information, description and humour:

At Salisbury Fair, among the sights and sounds. A person passing through the Market Square today would hardly realise, in the garb of peace and quietness it now wears, that it was, during the first three days of the week, the scene of a queer mixture of confusion, noise, and delight, which are its characteristics during the annual pleasure fair. If you were to ask the youngsters, who have lightened the weight of their money-boxes with rides on the hobby-horses, or in beholding the marvels of the waxworks, or who have a confused idea of 'music' emitted from the discordant orchestra of wailing and blaring organs, they would probably tell you that never was there such a glorious gala in the history of the world.

But if you were to speak to those who have watched the progress and decline of the Salisbury Fair year after year, and are therefore entitled to give an idea on the subject, you would listen to the universal opinion that this year's fair was not to be compared with that of previous years – though not much worse than last. The only difference of view would be that whereas some with a sneaking regard for old time amusements – and the writer pleads guilty to being in that category – would sigh and regretfully murmur 'Worse luck', whilst others, with a gleam of satisfaction in their eyes, would exclaim, 'The fair is dying out, and a good job too'.

But the purpose of this article, for the moment, is not to deal with regrets for the past or speculations as to the future. For though some of us cannot help looking upon the din created in the proximity of a leading business part of the city as an intolerable nuisance, yet there is associated with the round of pleasure a certain charm which cannot be resisted. It was in vain that the writer determined the other night to reach Castle Street from Fisherton Street by the circuitous route of round Silver Street, the Canal, Milford Street, Brown Street, Rollestone Street, Salt Lane and Scots Lane, in order to be far from the madding crowd. When he reached the vicinity of St Thomas' Church, some irresistible impulse drew him round by the 'drangway'. A moment or so later he was in the thick of the 'fun of the fair', and he would not perjure himself by saying he was altogether disappointed.

It was an animating scene, in sooth. The gorgeously

Looking down from Salisbury Cathedral nave roof.

decked proscenium of the waxwork show, the glitter of gaudy colour on the switchbacks and roundabouts, the drolleries of the showmen straining their lungs as they touted for customers, the brazen-throated organs grinding away simultaneously at different tunes with deafening discord, the roar of the multitude in the square, the shouts of half merriment and half fear of some of the youngsters (aye, and some old'uns, too) as they swirled round the undulating track of the aerial railroad, or galloped around the endless circle on the, 'firey untamed steeds', that bobbed up and down with the semblance of racing, as they spun onward to the 'music' which we have before mentioned but have not attempted to describe – all these things, combined, produced upon the mind a nameless bewilderment of delight.

The first thought was one of pity for the unfortunate tradesmen whose places of business this hubbub was in the very midst of, but that was, after all, supplanted by a stranger feeling of gratification of the fact that it seemed to be the means of giving hearty and earnest enjoyment to hundreds of folks who perhaps never have any other chance of obtaining it. Those who can find a warm corner in their hearts for the little ones, must have been in a state of high pleasure at the evidences presented of the delights in which the youngsters were positively revelling. Never to them did sweets taste so dainty of flavour as those bought by a thoughtful parent at one of the many stalls; never were toys hugged so closely to the little breasts, with a sense of anxious pleasure; never was man so funny as the droll clown who fooled and capered on the platform outside the show; never were wonders so great and marvellous as those to be seen inside the show; and never did the little heads whirl so much with the intoxication of the babel and pandemonium of delight.

It was thus that the juvenile mind was struck, the children of older growth did not fail to recognize in the fair the usual elements of comicality. It is true, we suppose, that a man on pleasure bent can extract humour from almost anything. In the ordinary course, there is nothing diverting in the extraction of corns – especially when personally struggling with an old and longstanding friend and adherent – and one does not always laugh at the administration of medicine. But the crowd who thronged round the chiropodist in the Market Square, who had extracted corns 'from all the crowned heads of Europe' (though he probably meant their feet) – and watched his operations on customers from among the throng, could not help laughing, partly because there was something droll about the operations, and partly because they were 'out to enjoy themselves' and must laugh, whether they would or not. The quack doctor, too, did a brisk trade, but perhaps with him his wonderful volubility and terror-striking vocabulary of expressions proved the greatest attraction.

But oh! the watch seller! What a lot of infantile credulity there is in the pleasure-seeking British public! To think that there are people gullable enough to imagine that for the twentieth part of the value of a Waterbury they can get a brand new English gold lever! Yet, by remarkable dexterity and bamboozling, the 'auctioneer' throws his line, the credulous fish (with a readiness that would shock the hungriest Avon trout) swallow the baited hook and part with their shillings. When the time is ripe the gold levers are distributed, a moment later the trick is discovered, the crowd roars with merriment, and the victims throw their gilded cases of useless tin on the ground, and dance on them with vexation.

At the boxing booths, too, similar scenes are enacted. A broad, burly-looking customer makes his appearance, and in a voice, as loud as his hide was apparently thick, challenges the world of pugilism to combat, and would give worlds to have only a round or two with Sullivan or Slavin or Corbett (or 'any of the lot'). The knot of lookers-on are awe-stricken – nobody dares take up the gauntlet and face so terrible an individual. The consequence is that the spectators are outside and not in, and business for the moment looks bad.

Just, however, as the crowd begins to move away in disappointment, a very little man (supposed to be from the country, but really an accomplice) suddenly presents his wiry form and breathes defiance to the challenger.

'Look 'ere, young man,' says the latter, 'I would advise yer to go home and ax yer mammy ter whack yer. I could lay sich as you with the tip of my little finger.'

'Could yer', says the supposed 'yokel' in a tone of assumed anger and disgust, 'Try it on, yer great bully, and let's see.'

'Go on away, lad, go away,' says the other deprecatingly, 'I want to fight men and not boys, but if yer doant mind coming inside I'll box yer ears for 'ee, just to satisfy yer.'

'I can't stand these hinsults any longer,' says the 'abused' one and rushes into the booth with a veritable leap, and the crowd flock in after him, expecting to be the witnesses of a fine piece of impromptu, but really carefully rehearsed, fun.

In the midst of so much robust enjoyment there are very few causes of complaint, the chief of these being that that execrable nuisance, the 'squirt', or 'Lady's teaser', as it is sometimes called, was in evidence during the fair. The police cannot be expected to do everything and be everywhere at the same time – indeed, they kept admirable order, thanks to Mr Matthews' capital arrangements. But it is really to be hoped that another year steps will be taken to put down the pest, which would soon have an ending, if the plan were adopted in Salisbury, which is in vogue in other places, viz., that of prosecuting both those who use and those who sell the abominations. It only remains to be added that the fair people cleared out on Thursday afternoon, and that the Square now wears its wonted appearance.

Personally, my sympathies are with the chiropodist. 'Crowned feet of Europe' just wouldn't have sounded right. But notice how carefully the essay has been constructed, and how well the writer has struck his course between serious comment and frivolity. Only at the end, when advocating the prosecution of water-pistol vendors, does the conventional Victorian psyche put in an appearance.

But, at the risk of labouring a point, I must make two more

observations in favour of this piece. The first is that deep under-currents lie beneath it. A royal commission had sat in Salisbury four years earlier to take evidence about the fair, and many harsh words and dire predictions were made about it. There were calls that it should be abolished.

The second, quite different, point is that a short story by Thomas Hardy, 'On the Western Circuit' (which was probably written in 1891 and was published in 1894), uses Salisbury Michaelmas fair as its backcloth. The present essay, we recall, dates from 1892. I find it intriguing to read the two descriptions, and imagine that perhaps Hardy and our anonymous reporter unconsciously brushed past each other in the 'madding' crowd, as both their heads bristled with the words they needed to transfer the scene to paper.

*　　*　　*

Curiouser and curiouser

The popular culture of the Victorian funfair had evolved over centuries, and details had been carried by local newspapers since they were first printed. Here is a notice about a forthcoming fair, and dates from 1774:

> INTELLIGENCE EXTRAORDINARY: As the 25th of September happens this year on a Sunday, Shrewton Fair will be held on Monday the 26th instant; there will be the usual entertainments, but the nobility and gentry are in expectation of a Fete Champetre, where masks are to be admitted: We hear, a Miller in Plush will make the first appearance, and shew some odd tricks; but will be greatly outdone by one in a short fustian jacket, who will dance an hornpipe on a furze faggot from France, with ten thousand five hundredweight on his head: he will be introduced by a little Doctor, who will read a lecture on silence. – Some pretty diversions will be shewn by a man at Hyde and Seek; – A laughing figure in the shape of a Pumpkin, will bring all sorts of hot-house productions, and a sprig of the old tulip

tree in a tray, made of the famous Damory Oak; he will try
to make a Greyhound swallow a purse of guineas. The
company will all be entertained with blamange and plenty
of French wines – Franky Peggs, in the chair. NB. The roads
are made very good.

Strange the things which pass for entertainment, and
grotesque some of the food on offer:

On Tuesday evening last one Scarlet, a noted cock-fighter,
at Burbage, in this county, eat [i.e. ate], at an inn in
Marlborough, a raw cock, of 4 lb weight, which had been
killed that day in fighting. He eat it with bread, pepper, salt
and vinegar. After Scarlet had done, another canibal, his
companion, eat a cock of 5 lb weight, without any bread. The
latter, worse than savage, not content with displaying his
first brutish feats, afterwards eat a raw rat that had been
dead four days.

*   *   *

Up to no good

That was in 1773, according to James Waylen, who pasted the
cutting into his scrapbook. And if you think that that was unpleasant, just listen to what went on, according to the Clerk of the Works,
after the Whitsun Fair in Salisbury Cathedral Close:

And here it may not be foreign to the subject, to mention
a custom, which had prevailed time immemorial, because
the consequences of it must contribute to the fractures here
mentioned; viz. in the Whitsun holidays, a fair is kept within
the Close of Sarum, at which time it is customary for people
to go upon the spire, there having been sometimes upon it
eight or ten persons at a time.
The late bishop, dean and chapter, put a stop to these
fool-hardy practices, by which many lives were hazarded
without the least advantage to those who attempted it: and

the danger was the greater, because these people never went up but when heated with liquor, which furnished them with that unnecessary courage. It seems they had certain sports in their passage up and down, viz. those who were the highest had the pleasure of discharging their urine on those below. Whoever considers the effect of urine upon lead, stone, and timber, as likewise upon all materials used in buildings, will own, that a great mischief must ensue, and hasten the natural decays. Besides this, there is reason to suppose, that the weather door and some of the eight doors were left open, and so the rain and snow was conveyed into the very connections of the timber, and the iron that was to assist and strengthen the joints. There was always, at these times, another injurious practice, viz. that of people rambling all over the roofs of the church, and particularly in the gutters, where, besides their usual discharges, they frequently cut their names, the date of the time, and other foolish devices; and by vying who should make the deepest impressions, they frequently cut through the lead, and of course the water was let in upon the timbers, and hastened their decay.

D i a l e c t

'Leabourin' volk'

How uncouth they were, the Wiltshire peasantry! That, at least, is the impression we are given by the commentators of the day. But they, of course, were looking down on popular culture as something inferior and laughable. And we are in danger of making their prejudice our own.

Ten years ago I edited a little book of Edward Slow's dialect verse. He was a carriage-builder in Wilton, who rose to become the town's mayor and a respected alderman. During the 1860s, as a young man, he discovered an aptitude for writing dialect; and between 1864 and 1918, a few years before his death, he was the author of at least thirty-five small books and pamphlets, in dialect verse and prose.

By no stretch of the imagination can his work be described as great literature, or even good poetry. But the historical interest of his productions lies in the fact, as I wrote in my introduction, that he was no mere observer, but a participant in the things he described. 'And, unlike most writers of humble origins, he did not try to rise from the ranks of the working classes, or... try to interpret working-class ways to his intellectual friends.' He was writing for the 'leabourin volk', of whom he was one.

One of the poems which I included was 'Ower Girt Zeptember Vair'. It paints an evocative picture of Wilton sheep fair, in a way quite different from the journalist's account of Salisbury fair. Here is part of his treatment of the quack orator:

> *Zee yonder Quack begins his clack,*
> *Like a maniac he spouts till he's black;*
> *Zays he, mines tha tack,*
> *If ya've pains in tha back,*

Ar any wur else, I'll cure tha attack
Why do ee remain za long in yer pain,
Wen I stoutly maintain
That if you obtain my medicines plain
Good health you'll regain, yes! an retain,
An never agean complain;
Dwont think ta meak wills,
Bit teak my pills, and be rid of yer ills,
Eece an 'tis zaprisan, wieout disguisin,
Ow many putts vaith in thease Quacks advisin...

Edward Slow, as we saw in our first chapter, printed complimentary reviews of his work in some of his books. They were taken from various magazines and local newspapers, including the *Durham Chronicle, Court Circular, Middlesbrough News, Carriage Builders' Gazette*, and the *Richmond and Ripon Chronicle.* Presumably the reviews had been syndicated to these far-flung periodicals, and Slow did not actually send out complimentary copies all over the country.

Perhaps not, although we have it from Edith Olivier that he did send a copy to Alfred Lord Tennyson, because he felt that poets should always be ready to exchange their works. The poems of Tennyson duly arrived in return, with a note: 'I thank you for your meritorious volume of poems.' And I can testify to having found, in a second-hand bookshop in Ripon (one of the places from which reviews emanated), three small pamphlets of Slow's works, dating from 1902-6. One of them is so rare that I do not believe that it exists in any library in Wiltshire. Here is a short piece of dialect prose from it:

TRAVELLEN ATHOUT AR TICKET. When tha new Zouth Waastern Railway wur aupend vrim Zalsbury ta Wilton [in 1859], there wur a main lot a Wilton bwoys as wur prentices in tha Zity, who waaked backurds an verreds nite and marnen; zometimes some on ess manidged ta muster up the tuppence apeny ta pay var a ride in tha train, which wur conzidered a bit of a luxury, an a girt trate in thic em there days. Tha ticket collector at Zalsbury Stayshen wur a main crotchety zart of a feller, an a got it into he's yead that zome a we bwoys did offen av a ride in athout ar a ticket an slip out weout bein zeed. Bit twur never done as I knaas on, at laste I never tried it on. Houzemever just var a lark, an ta get thease yer jealus minded Collectors back up a bit, Ben Binks zaays ta I one marnen, jist loud anuff varn ta hear, 'Diss knaa Jack I da offen come vrim Wilton ta Zalsbury, athout ar a ticket'. The Collector hearen on it, collar'd un be tha ear, led un into tha Booken Office, and zent var tha Stayshen Measter; who axed what wur the matter. 'Why zur, zaays tha vussy Collector, I auveryears thease young scamp tell he's companion there, that he offen comes vrim Wilton ta Zalsbury athout ar a ticket'; 'Is that true', zays Stayshen Measter. 'Eece zur I do,' zaays Ben. 'Well how do you manidge ta do it?' says he. 'Why I da waak in,' zays Ben.

A coose Stayshen Measter cooden help smilin as a let ess bouath off. Bit thic ar Ticket Collector wur down on Ben an I, as longs he lived.

*   *   *

Edward Slow's Novel

Slow's undoubted talent for mimicking his own, and his friends', way of speaking brought him considerable local celebrity around the turn of the century. But in his largest and most ambitious project I cannot help the feeling that he overreached his abilities. This was a full-length novel of 260 pages, *Jan Ridley's New Wife*, and was published in 1913. The plot is thin and contrived, and the characters only appear in order to serve as mouthpieces for Slow's attempt to contrast Wiltshire and Cockney dialects, with a dose of public-school English thrown in for good measure. In this extract a picnic is about to take place at a well known national monument about ten miles from Wilton:

Well, upon my sacred wod and honnah,' says Dick [a Cockney], 'these are really some monsters and naow mistike! I've seen a few big blocks of stoan in my time at various plices in

London, but, by jove, these giants beat em oll holler, anyhaow. And the puzzle of it is, Tribbet, how in the nime of thunder did they get em heah, seeing there were no railroads or machinery either, when them hoff-civilized old fogies they call Druids fixed em up. Well, its a bloomin conundrum, that's what it is, and oll the learned and knowing ones as ever existed, who have studied em, examined em, and wrote abaht em, cawn't mike em out any more than you or I can. Well, as I syes, heah they aw, and heah I suppoas they'll remain, a bloomin mystery, and its naow use form you and me to puzzle our brains as to how they kime heah, or for what purpose they were fixed up; sow let's gow and have some inside lining, for I begin to feel a sinking just here,' says he, tapping the lower part of his waistcoat. 'This heah air down heah seems to set a fellow's innwards longing or something to do pretty often.' The party were soon busily engaged making short work of the ham sandwiches, bread, cheese, and ale. 'Upon my sacred wod and honnah,' says Dick, after he'd finished, 'never in oll my blessed life have I ever relished such a snack as that; them sandwiches were a real treat, and as for Uncle's hoam brewed ail, it's really like imbibing Moet's best sparkling Phizz.' 'Ah, it's tha hayer, my bwoy,' zays Jan Ridley [a Wiltshireman], 'ower good woold country vresh hayer; that's the zart a saace to go we yer grub, as da meak ee relish it zoo.'

'No doubt about that, Uncle,' says Tom Tribbet [a public-school type], 'for although your good, wholesome, homely fare is relishable anywhere and anywhen, yet when a fellow gets an appetite hightened and sharpened by this beautiful bracing air, it is doubly so.' 'Heah, heah!' says Mister Daisher, 'thems my sentiments exactly, Mister Tribbet.'

'What do ee think a tha Stounes, Dick?' zays Missus Ridley. 'Think of em, Haunt? Well, to sum it up quick, I think em a bloomin mystery as nobody ever have, or ever will unravel. What's the good of all them bookworm fellas, archeological and antiquarian, coming here, spoutin and lecturin, and suggestin this, that, and tother, and writin books and pamphlets about em enough to stock a library, and awfter oll, they knaow naow more abaht em than you or I do, Haunt; thats my private opinion. It's oll a matter of theory and speculation on their pawts.'

'I tell ee what it is,' zays Jan Ridley, 'I've a bin visitin thease yer Girt Big Stounes dozens a times, ever zunce I were a bwoy, at ael sazons a tha year, an at ael times, marnen, non an night. I've a studied em, rade about em, an dramed about em in bade an out a bade; run em auver in me mind in wirk an out a wirk; Zundys an week days, an atter ael this, I've come ta tha clusion that they were stuck up be the Devil, an nabiddy else, an twur about tha time as he wur draved out a Heaven be Zaint Michael, as we da rade about in Scripter. Atter bein turned out, ya zee, a diden knaa where ta goo, zoo at last a wandered ta Zalsbury Plaain, an stuck up thase yer Girt Stounes var a house ta bide in.' At this very quaint suggestion the company all burst out laughing. 'Well, ya mid ael laugh, bit now let's hear what you've got ta zay about em ar bit better, will ee?' zays he. 'Well, I for one,' says Tom Tribbet, 'certainly lean to the prevailing opinion, that, they were erected by the Druids as a Temple to worship the Sun, for as you're aware, even to this day, on the 21st of every June, the summer solstice, people come from all parts to see that luminary cast it's first ray on rising, across the 'Friar's Heel' yonder, on to the Altar Stone just here.'

Yes, writing dialogue is a gift not given to us all; and the confusion is only made worse when, as you may have noticed, the narrator keeps changing his accent as well. But if that took you a long time to read, I can assure you that it took a great deal longer to type into my word processor. Spare a thought for the printer's poor compositor who in 1913 had to set the whole book.

*   *   *

A *Parish on Wheels*

Having seen how not to do it, let us turn to someone who did it rather well. Howard Swinstead was a priest employed by Salisbury Diocese from 1892-5 as itinerant minister to the gipsies and travelling population of the area, and in 1897 he published an account of his work, which he called *A Parish on Wheels*. It is a scarce book which I have never seen anyone refer to, so I propose to give it an airing. In this passage Swinstead describes a theme by now familiar to us, the activities of the quack orator at a country fair:

His complete kit is a shiny hand-bag, containing illustrations on calico of dreadful fractures to limb and skull, and oddments. These are spread before him, with mysterious precision, guarded by a bottle or two, which the orator by turns patrols and handles with affection.

During these ostentatious preliminaries a small audience of velveteens and sky-blue ties assembles.

The speaker delivers himself with slow, deliberate, perhaps bibulous, hauteur, as if he expects to catch a new auditor with every syllable.

'My name is Pro-fessor Chunk, chiropodist and taxidermist' (the nearest listeners look terror-stricken as the orator clears his throat). 'In order to ass-ure you, ladies and gentlemen (the gentler sex are entirely imaginary), that I am not a quack, but a bonyfide 'erbalist of twenty years' study and standin', I will give you my card stating the postal address, to which letters of hevery description will be delivered – if correctly addressed – to me by her Majesty's post officials: Pro-fessor H. Chunk, General Practitioner and Bird-fancier, Yeovil Road, Sherborne.

'The reason for which I have the honour of addressing you in this field to-day is, as you will see, owing to the loss of my arm from causes connected with my past 'istory.' (Here he puts his whole conceited soul into the narration, and if he lacks an arm, his eyes do their best to dilate and make up for the loss.) 'I was a faithful soldier in her Majesty's service in the Ashanti Campaign in the year 1870, and it was my privilege to lose my arm for my Queen and country while dashin' heroically at the black but comical enemies of our nation. Their 'air was made of feathers. But they scraped my arm off, I will give them that credit, and retired ignerminously defeated.'

(How often have I wished that I could arrest and keep my congregation's attention as this man did; but perhaps his subject permitted of the more varied treatment and the less exactness of statement.)

'Since that date, my friends and fellow-countrymen, I have been withdrawn from active service, and therefore you see me now living still to benefit my nation. It is to do you all good that I came. Now, I am prepared, by means of this compound of 'erbs, which I now 'old between my forefinger and thumb, labelled with my hown trademark on each bottle, which will cure all the natural ailments that the body is suffering – except a broken leg. Stand back, if you please.!

'And so, if any gentleman here is afflicted with rheumatism, asthma, gout, peritonitis, neuralgia, or a slow liver, he has only to give me current coin to the amount of one shilling and a penny halfpenny (by post to the registered address, threepence more), and he will receive instant attention from headquarters, who will send him this bottle. I have only a dozen, so be quick, if you want them now; the chief ingredient is *aqua pura cum grano salis*, which, if taken in large enough quantities, will relieve anyone of indigestion caused by too liberal feeding at his last meal. (All right, young man, you can 'ear just as well if you step back off my dispensary carpet. Thank *you!*)

'I was myself troubled with excrescences on the chin; my barber allowed this razor to go through these, instead of passing over them. The result was apocryphal: the blood was abysmal, and the warts were quite irreplaceable.

'But if any gentleman 'ere is covered from 'ead to foot with bubukles, whelks, or pimples, let him step forward, and with my elixir for the preservation of the cuticle in all forms, I will cure him.'

(The challenge is not accepted.)

'There was a lady come to me last week, tremblin' with beauty like the flower-garden in her 'at. And I said to her, "Good madam, pray be seated – and how are you? Have you taken the medicine I gave you?" She replied, "I am takin' it. I am as I am, and I can't be no ammer." Now that, I conceive, is the right spirit in which to take medicine.

'Do your best and leave the rest with Nature. (A wave of pious but resigned approval here passed over the faces of the bystanders.)

'You say you believe in my medicines (this was quite gratuitous as a true quotation, for no one had opened his lips). Well, I reply, believe in them one and three halfpence. Thank you, sir – only one bottle, you said? And you another? Yes: you don't look too well, my lad; try two doses at a time, and then send for more when you've finished – that's what you want, and so do I.'

I knew not how near I was to danger while being entertained by this stranger unawares.

'Won't you come and see a great curiosity I have, sir? It is marvellous; we only show it to a few gentlemen quite private – not a public show.'

With that he led me into a frail booth, whose calico walls flapped feebly in the wind, and with great show of doing me an enormous kindness in the strictest secrecy, he unlocked one box after another, until he produced the most degrading and nauseating show I have ever been entrapped into seeing.

'What do you think of it, sir? isn't it marvellous?'

'Yes, I allow that; but –'

He was off, had mounted the steps in front of the booth, signalled silence to the man who had by banjo beguiled a wavering audience to pause and look at nothing particular, gave the assistant the keys to lock up his show, and just as I came out of the curtained entrance, shouted in a raucous voice:

'The clergyman who is now standin' before you at the entrance to my show declares it is the most marvellous and soul-stirrin' sight he ever beheld. It is a reg'lar tail-twister! He is from the Bishop of Salisbury, and all the clergy and noblemen of the county agree with his recommendation that I have now to show you,' etc. – but by this time I was quite out of earshot.

He afterwards replied to my remonstrances:

'Well, you see, sir, public speakers like you and me – we has to gull the public, hasn't we, sometimes?'

But I got 'upsides wi' un" within three months. It was to an August crowd under the Weymouth Jubilee Clock that he was spouting his first-quoted moving address (or something like it), when he spied me coming along, and with great gusto appealed to me for a recommendation of his goods.

'There's a gentleman – a clergyman too – will tell yer the same.'

Several heads turned my way in the direction indicated by his demonstrant finger, and by an inspiration which has always since seemed unaccountable, I turned my own head with the rest, to look for the advertisement he was pointing out.

The effect was a most desirable one: the unpaid advertisement fell flat, the public felt duped, and I chuckled at the score paid off three months after date.

L o s t   C a u s e s

The Art of Flying

The Salisbury Diocese Itinerant Mission continued for another twenty years after Swinstead had left it, but seems to have been killed off by the First World War. Its work was highly regarded by both churchmen and travellers.

But the clergy's brushes with itinerants and wonder workers had not always been so cordial. Here is part of a letter about an event which occurred in a village near Devizes in 1735:

> Mankind, not satisfied with travelling on the elements of earth and water, have attempted to invade the air, from the days of Daedalus downwards. 'Pennis non homini datis', ('with wings not given to man') they have hitherto essayed, unsuccessfully, the Art of Flying: notwithstanding Bishop Wilkins's prediction that the time would come when a man setting out on a journey would ring for his wings, as heretofore for his boots.
>
> About 100 years ago, an adventurer of this kind travelled the country, making for money at different places the exhibition of a flight from towers and steeples. His method was to have a rope fixed to the top of the place from which he was to descend, and strained to a convenient place where he was to alight. A board, with a groove to receive the cord, was fixed to the breast of the 'aeronaut', and by this he was to descend headforemost to the point of alighting. Amongst other places he visited Bromham, and having solicited permission to 'fly' from the steeple, some idle people of the place, without consulting the clergyman, who was indisposed, gave him leave to perform. A time was appointed, the apparatus was fixed, and a mob assembled. The flyer ascended

the steeple, made his plunge, and was half way down the rope, when some persons employed to strain it pulled it too hard. The top of the spire gave way, and came down. The aeronaut, luckily for himself, fell into a tree in the churchyard, and received but little hurt. Had he fallen to the ground he would have been dashed to pieces. This event probably put an end to steeple-flying; but as the inhabitants of a country are often ridiculed for the foolish acts of their neighbours, the story of pulling down their own steeple was for a long time a standing joke against the people of Bromham. It was repaired; but some years afterwards was struck by lightning, and shivered near the same point where it had been broken before.

Bromham Church

The Wiltshire Coalfields

The pages of history, of course, are littered with human follies of every kind, and I had long been intrigued by a reference I came across in Dr. Hunnisett's edition of eighteenth-century Wiltshire coroners' inquests. On 6th May 1776 at Longbridge Deverill (near Warminster), we are told:

> Thomas Coward was in the bottom of a pit digging for coal and had just sent up a thing full of earth called by the miners a cart when the rope broke and let fall the cart and earth with great violence and killed him on the spot.

But why should he have been digging for coal at Longbridge Deverill? The parish lies on chalk and greensand, with the Oxford clay outcropping not far away at Horningsham. But the nearest coalfield is in the Radstock area, nearly fifteen miles away, and the coal measures at Longbridge Deverill must be thousands of feet underground. The mystery remained, until I came across a short article by Professor J. Buckman, entitled, 'On some coal mining operations at Malmesbury', which was published in 1855:

> The little town of Malmesbury is well-known to the anti-quary for the remains of its once glorious abbey, its interesting market-cross, and, if I recollect rightly, a cozy hostel, formed out of the ruins of an old conventual building, besides other reliques of great interest. Its inhabitants are a primitive race who derive great satisfaction from a charter, and still better, from a large piece of rich land bequeathed to them by King Athelstan. Now, whether the king with his bequest gave the assurance that, by digging deep, those into whose hands the said land might fall would realize great treasure, or whether some person in digging a well suddenly came upon a black coaly-looking substance in the stratum of clay, does not appear; but we incline to the latter opinion. However this may be, certain it is, that about a century ago, operations for coal-mining were commenced on Malmesbury Common; the timber of the estate was felled to pay the expenses of

a shaft that was sunk and, as report said, coal found. Indeed this latter assertion had been verified over and over again, as young natural philosophers (and they were very young in it) had from time to time collected lumps of carbonaceous matter, black as coal, and which on being brought to the unerring test of experiment – the trial by fire – burnt like coal; in short, were the true 'black diamond'.

Still with this evidence the mining had been abandoned after the sinking of a shaft – and of some money. The latter article, by the way, was supposed to have been raised again by the wary ones whom rumour asserted to have been bought over not to prosecute the work any farther by the coal-masters of another district, in order to prevent the competition which this new mine from its contemplated riches must inevitably produce. Now as this opinion still prevailed, it was not long since deemed advisable to re-investigate the matter, but this time it was determined that such investigation should be intrusted to a geologist, and as such I was requested to undertake the inquiry.

Having therefore gone to this most interesting district to prosecute my mission, I was soon in communication with some intelligent gentlemen who represented the estate, when the evidence connected with the opening of the shaft was laid before me. About two pounds weight of the previously-mentioned black substance brought from the shaft, was submitted for inspection. This black matter of course proved to be lignite or carbonized wood, thin deposits of which will be found in most thick clay deposits, and very frequent in this which is the Oxford clay. Such appearances, however, have frequently led to fruitless mining experiments, the usual argument for which is, 'here is a good burning coal got a few feet from the surface; it is true it is but a thin seam, but how much thicker will it become the deeper we descend.

On going to the site of the old shaft, I soon found that it had been commenced in the Oxford clay formation, and from examining the exposed debris of the shaft, I became convinced that the opening of nearly one hundred yards in depth as stated by my guide, had not pierced through the Oxford clay bed.

Here, then, the question of obtaining coal on this spot was at once set at rest, inasmuch as we should have many thick formations to penetrate before arriving at the usual position of coal-bearing beds. [Since] the aggregate thickness... would not fall far short of 3,000 yards,... it became evident that it would be rash in the extreme to recommend any operations in search of coal, as even if it were proved to exist... it would be far beyond a mining depth, and besides we are quite without evidence of its quantity or value.

'He that diggeth a pit, shall fall into it,' we are told in the Bible. Many of the pits which people dig for themselves are less spectacular than that which disappointed the 'primitive race' of Malmesbury (I must say, by the way, that I have always found them most hospitable and sophisticated); nor are they so traumatic as the pit which carried off Thomas Coward.

*   *   *

A Cracked Existence, or ... Swindon is flat

But the most heroic champions of lost causes are those who, having been proved to be misguided, persist in their beliefs. One such who never flinched from defending his philosophy was John Hampden. The *Swindon Advertiser* takes up the story:

What first brought Mr Hampden to Swindon was never generally known. What was known was this. He came with the remnants of issues of a number of pamphlets he had published crammed into boxes and other receptacles, and also with his pockets and hands full of copy of other pamphlets he wanted to publish. Shortly previous to Mr Hampden's advent, Swindon had been visited by another pamphleteer and lecturer; one who had sought to tell the public something new by disputing the old theory of the world's rotundity through the medium of a lecture, followed by the sale of a book in which the whole proofs were to be seen at a glance. Like many another venturesome adventurer, this gentleman met with such ill success at Swindon that he could not pay for his printing in cash, and he therefore paid for it in kind. The printer took out his bill in his customer's books. When John Hampden appeared the printer sought to turn one of the books into cash by inducing him to become a purchaser. John Hampden bought the book, and the circumstance became the turning point in what at best had been but a cracked existence. He became positively cranky over the credulity of mankind in believing that the earth was round and not flat. He at once abandoned all his old studies and theories. Old pamphlets and new copy all went into the fire or elsewhere, and from that moment onward John Hampden went forth, like another Don Quixote refreshed, with the Swindon printer doing duty as his Sancho Panza, to maintain the great truth of the age – the earth is flat and not round. Hitherto John Hampden had lived an ideal life in the realms of theory. He was a student, we have been told, of prophecy, and the purpose of most of his voluminous pamphlets and fly sheets had been to prove from the Jewish prophet Daniel that the termination of the times of the Gentiles would come shortly, when the second advent of Christ takes place, and the Jews with the lost ten tribes are restored to their pre-eminence as a nation at Jerusalem. He looked for startling events between 1891 and 1894.

In fact, a truly startling event (for him) did occur towards the end of January 1891. He died.

Here is his obituary, from the *Wilts and Gloucestershire Standard:*

The death is announced of a well-known former resident in Swindon, and at one time a frequent contributor to our columns, Mr. John Hampden. The death of Mr. Hampden, says the Standard, of Wednesday last, the sturdy upholder of the theory that our earth is flat, if it has no other effect on the world at large, will at least be a distinct loss to the

Postal revenue. For his correspondence, if rather one-sided, was unwearied. No astronomer of any eminence but has, at some period of his career, been favoured with a more or less abusive missive, and though these 'demonstrations of their ignorance' were never answered, the fact in no way cooled Mr.Hampden's ardour. For, if silence did not give consent, passive resistance to his arguments regarding the flatness of the earth, and unfulfilled prophecies, were accepted as proofs that his 'facts' were unanswerable. Some savants, indeed, were singled out for peculiar distinction. They had pamphlets, and even little volumes, penned to their dishonour. 'Ignorance', 'credulity', 'deliberate attempts to deceive a trusting world' — such were the mildest of the charges which were brought against the teachers of the accepted system of cosmogony. Now and then, indeed, when the turpitude of believing in the rotundity of the earth became more than usually intolerable, Mr.Hampden issued a special journal to denounce the knavishness of the latest 'Newtonian impostor'. His life was devoted to such kicking against the pricks, and the saddest feature in this worthy man's delusion was that he firmly believed in the truth of his paradox, which is, perhaps, more than could be said of some who pandered to his harmless craze.

In private life Mr.Hampden is understood to have been a reasonable person, and as a man of business, endowed with decided acuteness. But once touch, in even the remotest manner, on the 'so-called' oblate-spheroidicity of the earth, and you were doomed to a verbal avalanche. Yet it is erroneous to suppose that Mr.Hampden was the inventor of that exploded hypothesis. Though his writings were most numerous, and his map, with the North Pole in the centre of a plain, and the South Pole running all around it, was best known, it was another paradoxist, writing and lecturing under the name of 'Parallax', who first led Mr.Hampden into the error, which cost him so much time and money, and, one might think, worry, were it not certain that controversy in which the talk was all on one side was the salt of his life. 'Parallax' was a surgeon in North London, and though he died a few years ago without abjuring his absurdities, it is always doubtful how far Mr. Samuel Rowbotham quite swallowed his oft-exploded arguments.

But just as the inquiring intellect of Sir Richard Phillips, bereft of sufficient knowledge to keep its speculation within reasonable bounds, was a victim to the paradox in his day, so Mr. Hampden, who then lived at Swindon, found something attractive in the specious talk of the latest earth-flattener. But what was worse still, he accepted in an unquestioning spirit the experimental basis of 'Parallax's' theory, that on a part of the Bedford Canal where there is an uninterrupted water line of about six miles, the fullest tests had proved that there were no signs of curvature. Unfortunately for Mr. Hampden, he wagered five hundred pounds on his opinion as to the correctness of this statement, which, if true, would have gone some little way to substantiate a view negatived, however, by a score of far more conclusive facts. And the result was that, though he remained as unbelieving as ever, he lost his five hundred pounds, and got himself into endless trouble.

An eminent naturalist, in fact, accepted his challenge, and 'staked' the money with the conductor of a sporting journal. Perhaps it would have been wiser to have refused to degrade a scientific question to the level of a vulgar bet; since no one whose opinion was worth considering was at all likely to espouse Mr. Hampden's heresy. However, three boats were moored in a line, three miles or so apart. Each carried a mast of a given length, the conditions of the experiment being that if, when the tops of the first and last masts were seen in a line through a telescope, the summit of the middle mast was not found to be above the level, the earth-flattener was to be adjudged the money. The result may be anticipated. Mr. Hampden returned from 'the Level' a poorer, but not a wiser man. On the contrary, his wrath knew no bounds; but, instead of expending his indignation on the paradoxer who had led him astray, he devoted it to those who 'still believed' in the earth's rotundity. The subsequent history of the affair was, indeed, extremely unpleasant, for it landed the loser in the Law Courts, and estranged from him much of the sympathy which might otherwise have been bestowed on the ignorant victim of so unequal a contest. Mr. Hampden became plaitiff in an action to recover his five hundred pounds from the hands of the stakeholder, on the technical ground that the transaction was in the nature of a 'gaming or wagering contract', and, as such, null and void by the Statute 8 and 9 Vict. c.109 s.18. Upon this ground the late Lord Chief Justice Cockburn, and the late Justices Mellor and Quain, decided in favour of Mr. Hampden. Still, Mr. Hampden did not abate his ardour or spare his printer's ink; he went further, and added to his leading foible very pronounced views of the proper interpretation of the Book of Daniel. His mind was, in truth, so constituted that no facts could convince him of his error.

To such a damning indictment of a man's life-work there can be little to add, except to reveal that the 'eminent naturalist' was Alfred Russel Wallace (1823-1913), a most distinguished scientist and humanist, who many people credit with anticipating Darwin's theory of natural selection. The outcome of the 1870 experiment was in fact less clear-cut than Wallace had imagined, because Hampden insisted on using a theodolite rather than a telescope, and then interpreted the result differently. Successive bouts of litigation left Wallace a great deal poorer than the £500 he had wagered, and perhaps led him to modify his view on the stage within the evolutionary process occupied by Mr. Hampden.

*   *   *

But to us, passive observers a century and more later, it all seems to have been a storm in a teacup, just like James Bodman's dispute with his librarian, or the wife-swapping in Swindon market-place, or Lady O'Looney's epitaph, or the rhubarb in Waterworks Road, or... – None of it really matters, except to those of us who like to indulge in small talk.

Sources

NOTE: Frequently cited sources are abbreviated as follows: *WAM* = *Wiltshire Archaeological and Natural History Magazine*; W.Cuttings = Wiltshire Cuttings, in Wiltshire Archaeological and Natural History Society Library, Devizes; *WNQ* = *Wiltshire Notes & Queries*; WRO = Wiltshire Record Office. Books are cited in full on their first occurrence only; thereafter the author's surname and the date of publication only are cited.

INTO PRINT. Prefaces and other Mishaps: Duke, E., 1837, *Prolusiones historicae, or essays illustrative of the Halle of John Halle...*; *WAM*, 28, p.265; W.Cuttings, 3, p.9. A Librarian's Treachery: Bodman, J., 1814, *A concise history of Trowbridge...* (see also *WA&NHS Bi-Annual Bulletin*, 17, pp.11-12). All a Matter of Confidence: Bodman, 1814; Daniell, W., 1850, *Warminster Common...*; Morris, W., 1885, *Swindon fifty years ago...*; *WAM*, 28, pp.5-12. A Cynic: Davis, J., 1754, *Origines Divisianae, or the antiquities of the Devizes....* A Two-Edged Sword: Duke, 1837; Slow, E., 1899, *Humourous west countrie tales*. Envoi: Duke, 1837.

SUPERSTITIONS. A Donkey to the Rescue: Morris, 1885, pp.502-3; The Medicine Chest: *WAM*, 14, pp.325-6. Who needs a Doctor?: *WNQ*, 1, pp.167, 315, 317; *WNQ*, 2, p.242. Garden Warfare: *WNQ*, 4, pp.280-1. Rooted to the Spot: W.Cuttings, 3, p.6. Wilkinson's Questionnaire: WAS Library, Devizes. Oram's Grave: *WNQ*, 3, pp.275-6.

CLERGY. Broughton Gifford: WRO 501/1-2 (typed transcript by W.A. Webb in WAS Library, Devizes); *WAM*, 5, pp.267-341; *WAM*, 6, pp.11-72. A Temperate Vicar...: WRO 1505/32; WRO 1505/90; *Marlborough Times*, 6.9.1879, p.8. ...And an Intemperate Curate: Hunt, H., 1820, *Memoirs of Henry Hunt...*, vol.1, pp.189-92.

LIFE'S RICH TAPESTRY. Great Native Stamen: W.Cuttings, 3, p.36; *WNQ*, 3, pp.377-8; *WAM*, 17, 306-26; W.Cuttings, 3, p.18. Death's Rich Tapestry: Ravenshaw, T.F., 1878, *Antiente epitaphes* (see also *Notes and Queries*, 6th series, 2, pp.284-5; and W.Cuttings, 3, p.94); Bouverie, B.P., 1890, A *few facts concerning the parish of Pewsey...*, p.32; *WAM*, 28, pp.169-70. More Ham, less Calf: W.Cuttings, 3, p.103. Dabchicks, Gudgeons and Dogs: Gandy, I, 1975, *The heart of a village*, pp.16-17; Richardson, E., 1934, *Wiltshire folk*, pp.48-9, 102; *WNQ*, 2, pp.83-4; *WNQ*, 1, 129-30.

CRIME... The Darker Side of Cherhill: Blackford, J.H., 1941, *The manor and village of Cherhill*, pp.242-4; *WAM*, 24, pp.262-3. Mine Host: W.Cuttings, 3, p.3 (from *Wiltshire Gazette*, 13.1.1842). To Bournemouth for Tea: *WNQ*, 5, p.324. More

Problems on the Road: W.Cuttings, 3, pp.24, 14; *WNQ*, 4, p.278. Rising Again: Richardson, E., 1919, *The story of Purton...*, pp.50-2. A Poet who lost his Head: *WAM*, 29, pp.3-10.

...AND PUNISHMENT. A Gruesome Business: Britton, J., 1850, *The autobiography of John Britton*, vol.1, pp.36-7. More Hanging About: *WNQ*, 3, pp.333-4. Incident at Watkins' Corner: Richardson, 1934, pp.55-7. A Final Twist: Large, F., 1931, *A Swindon retrospect*, pp.55-6. Fiendish Devices: *WAM*, 1, pp.68-91. Coming round for more: *WAM*, 7, pp.1-44; *WNQ*, 1, pp.220-1. A Barbarous Villain: *WNQ*, 2, p.224. Salisbury Water Torture: W.Cuttings, 3, p.23. A Courtroom Drama: Jefferies, R., 1873, *Reporting, editing and authorship...*; various local newspapers, March—July, 1881.

NEWSPRINT. Unexpected Arrivals: Jefferies, 1873; *Swindon Advertiser*, 17.5.1869, p.2 (see also Silto, J., 1981, *A Swindon history, 1840-1901*, p.67, where it is misquoted); Buchanan, C.D., 1958, *Mixed blessing: the motor in Britain*, p.126; W.Cuttings, 1, p.29. Fillers: *Wiltshire Times*, 27.8.1881, p.8; *Trowbridge Chronicle*, 7.6.1879; W.Cuttings, 1, p.27. A Whiff of the Orient: *Trowbridge Chronicle*, 17.5.1879, p.6. The Rustic Polymath: *WNQ*, 1, pp.469-70. The Man in the Moon: *Trowbridge Chronicle*, various issues in 1883. More Trivia: *Wiltshire Times*, various issues, summer 1881.

FAIRS. Selling a Wife: Jefferies, 1873; Morris, 1885, pp.500-2. Salisbury Fair: W.Cuttings, 1, p.277. Curiouser and Curiouser: W.Cuttings, 3, pp.13, 12. Up to no Good: Price, F, 1774, *A description of that admirable structure the cathedral church of Salisbury...*, p.26.

DIALECT. 'Leabourin Volk': Chandler, J., 1982, *Figgetty pooden: the dialect verse of Edward Slow*; Slow, E., c.1903, *Humourous west countrie tales...*, p.37 (not to be confused with Slow, 1899, which has a similar title). Edward Slow's Novel: Slow, E., 1913, *Jan Ridley's new wife...*, pp.131-3. A Parish on Wheels: Swinstead, J.H., 1897, *A parish on wheels*, pp.212-16.

LOST CAUSES. The Art of Flying: *WAM*, 1. pp 351-2. The Wiltshire Coalfields: Hunnisett, R.F., 1981, *Wiltshire coroners' bills 1752-1796*, p.61 (Wiltshire Record Society, vol.36); *WAM*, 2, pp.159-61. A Cracked Existence, or... Swindon is Flat: *Swindon Advertiser*, 31.1.1891; *Wilts and Gloucestershire Standard*, 31.1.1891 (see also R. Schadewald, in *Smithsonian*, 4.1978).

I n d e x

Note: This is a selective index of persons, places and subjects, and omits many minor references.